Buckm n Journal 012:

# GORGE

Buckman Publishing LLC
est. 2018
1448 NE 28th Ave
Portland Oregon 97232
buckmanjournal.com

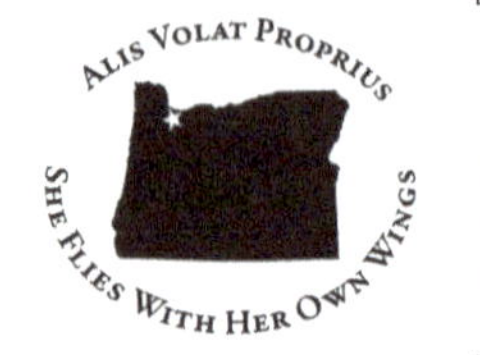


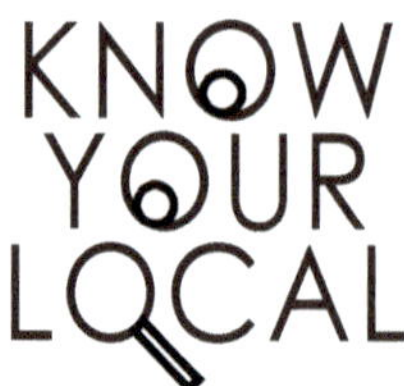


## Team Buck is:

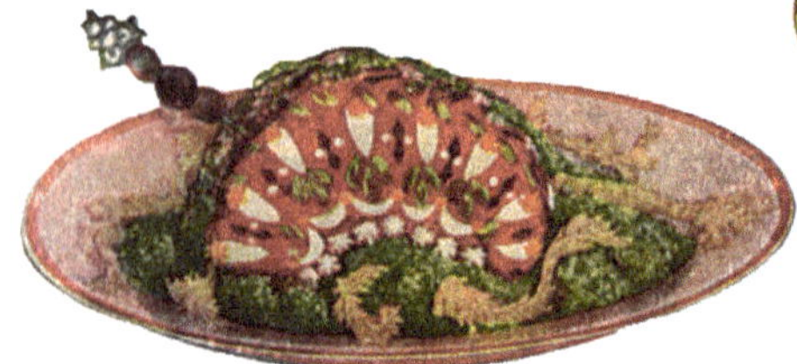

*Rich as "Corned Tongue in Aspic"*

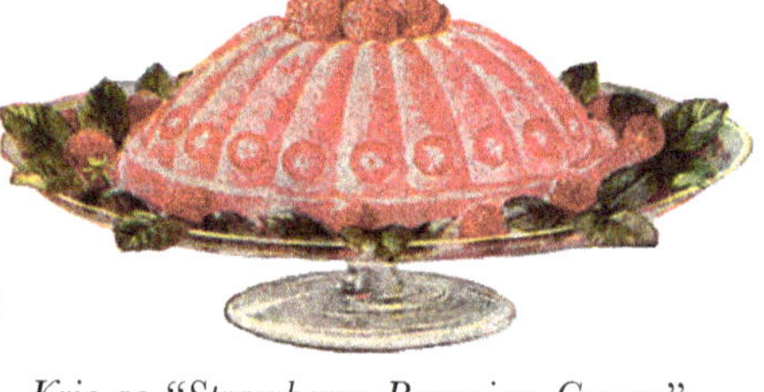

*Ellen as "Salmon Mold"*

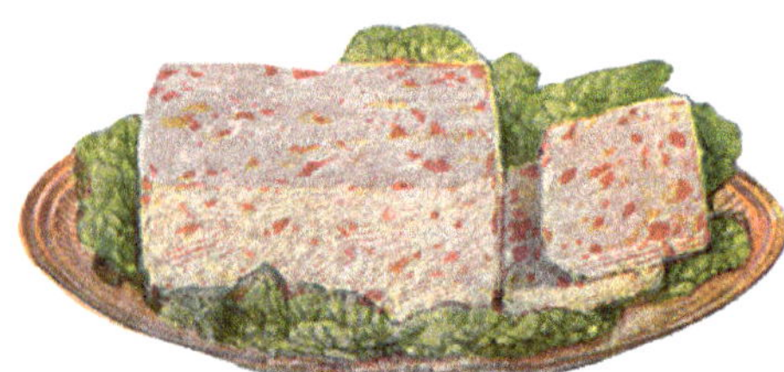

*Emmi as "Salad-Dessert"*

*Kris as "Strawberry Bavarian Cream"*

**Buck**
**mxn**

Congratulations! A Buckman production is in your hands! We're an unorthodox operation that continues the daredevil tradition of literature, printing new sparks that ignite imagination. Proudly independent, Buckman's defiant attitude aims to inspire and increase readership in greater society.

## Cover Info

Photography: Paisley Lee
Nail set & hand model: Sam Sangermano
Creative direction & styling: Ellen Robinette

## All Rights Reserved

# Dedicated to Ibby Rivers

Buckman has been the beneficiary of many groovy, talented folks in our six-year existence, but few have made more of a singular indentation on us than Ibby Rivers.[1] We published their illuminating collection, *Another Fortune & Other Poems* as one of our first book projects in 2019 and its words have only gotten wiser, juicier in the years since.

*Another Fortune live at Hallowed Halls* featured a beyond-genre collaborative performance of Ibby's poetry and the harp-work of musician Lily Breshears.[2] Included here are a few film photographs of that evening. Keep an ear out for the recording.[3] Hallowed indeed.

Let's keep their words aloft. The spirit going. We dedicate these, and really, all our pages from here on out to one of our dearest and most admired, Elizabeth Ibby Rivers. A true poet, queer innovator, studier of rocks and stars, wielder of clay and crowns-of-sonnets. We are your waters, forever.

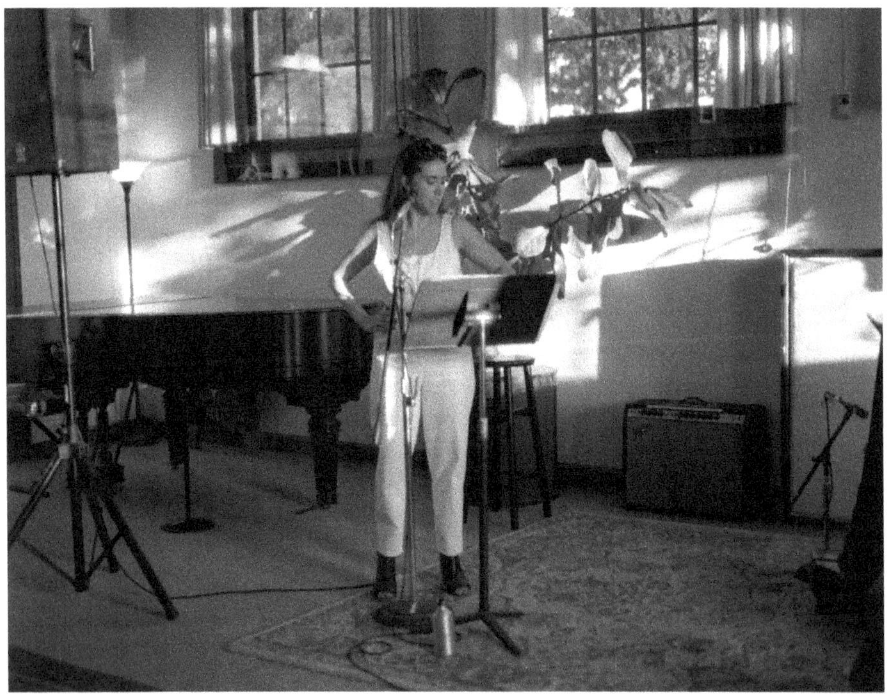


[1] *FKA Liz Lampman.*
[2] *The book also features illustrations from Lettie Jane Rennekamp.*
[3] *On the Buckman Journal website.*

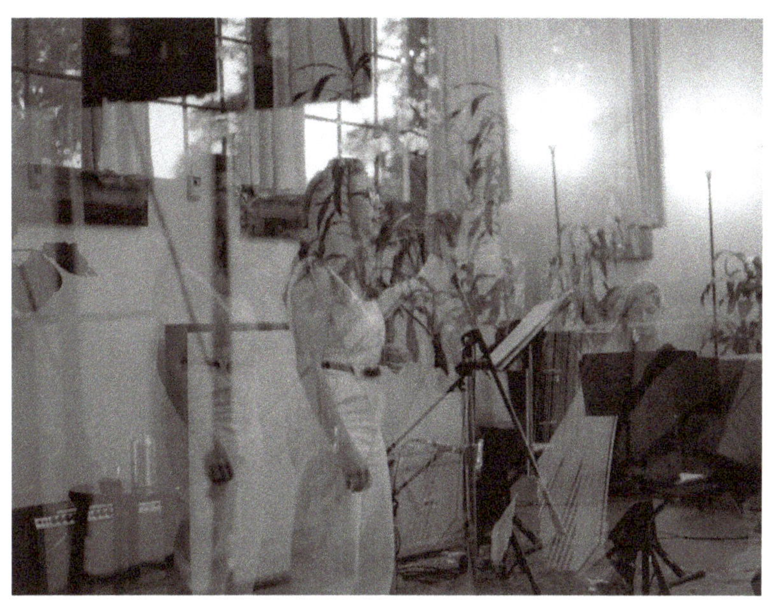

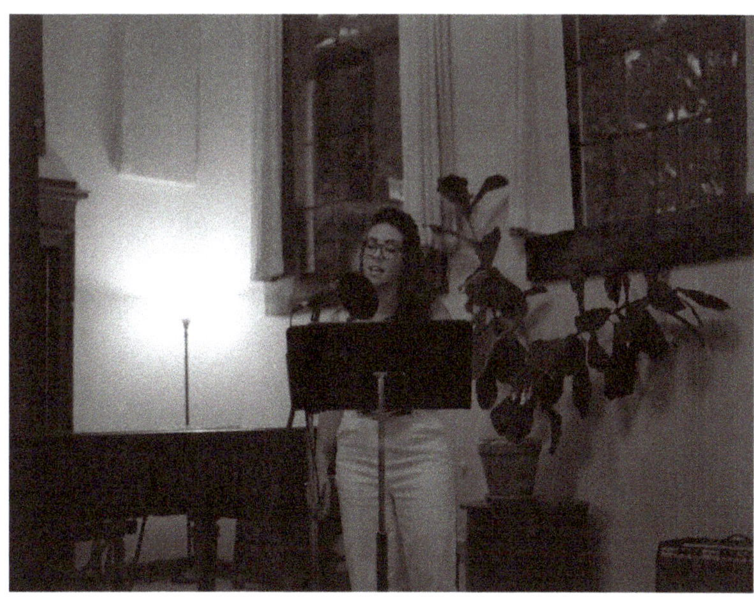

# Contents


**Letter from the Editor**
Collage by Zac Pranji
08

**About the Cover**
Photography by Paisley Lee
Nails by Sam Sangermano
10

**The Dive**
Fiction by Hannah Love
14

**Beach House**
Excerpt from an in-progress novel by S. Z. James
Photography by John Kirkley
20

**Ode to Creases**
Poetry by Andrew Simon
Sculpture by Alex Diamond
32

**CARVED**
Creative Non-Fiction by Jamie Cattanach
Drawing by Christian Johnson
38

**In the Mirror**
Comic by Ree Artemisa
52

**Minding the Gap: the Future of the Burnside Bridge**
Creative Non-Fiction by Anita Macauley
Photography by Goldandfaceted
54

**Venous Lake**
Flash Fiction by Tracey Nguyen
Mixed Media by Zac Pranji
70

**Such Golden Hours**
Excerpt from an in-progress novel by Dustin Hendrick
76

*The Institute of Living*
Adapted from an in-progress memoir by Sara Atwood
Collage by Kimberlee Frederick
84

*DEEPER*
Fiction by Noelle Smith
Printmaking by Claire Gunville
96

*a special case*
Poetry by Emily Moon
Drawing by Megan Chin
104

*Transplant*
Creative Non-Fiction by Jack Wang
Photography by Judy Jiang
110

*HAIL COLUMBIA!*
Poetry by Maxwell Kline

*Bleak Thrills*
Excerpt from a comic by Ree Artemisa
124

*Fractured Pangea*
Creative Non-Fiction by Alicia Johnson
Collage by Stephanie Hatch
126

*Last Ride of the Great Divide*
Fiction by Rich Perin
136

146 *Contributors*

*Honor Roll* 150

# Letter from the Editor

When was the last time you felt satiated, when you had as much as you could ever want? In the bank, in square feet, in nutrients, atmosphere? From birth, Capitalism instills the *best little consumer* ethos where every acquisition, every arriving, feels like it is just not, still not, never enough.

Derived from the Old French word for throat in the 13th century, *gorge* is understandably fleshy, vulnerable: proximity to river, to guts. Not only manifesting the want but devouring it down without boundary or end, breaknecking the desire path, gateless.

Like a lot of influential forces, this open-ended pursuit is a function of time. What is considered normal consumption only becomes surplus when occurring all in the span of a night or an hour. So maybe what we really want is a temporal gorge. Enough time to eventually have it all. If the accumulation could be infinite, then maybe so could you.

Get to know Gorge: short for gorgeous, the beauty spread when it's a little gross, even. The theory of the two a's touching. The blue pool coagulated, dripping.

Feeling all spiral? There's a bar for that; a special drink. If you're fed up with paying rent, there's a beach house commune for that. Hit up the dive, the ocean vent. The grief mirages, floating bits of continent. Consider the crossing, bridge as prism. Shapeshift for a smoky golden-age party, eat some revelatory beets—prelude of recovery. Witness the post-mortem of a confluence, bodies that crossed, emptied, diverged. Take a surreal swim in the Columbia, cross-continental-photo-etymology. Make the late-night scheme a reality.

The fire nightmare. Someone you smiled at. Overpowering the tastebuds. A half and quarter melon. The cables at your ankles, coming. The lakeland creases. The technicolor hills. Vegan diesel. Deep-space angels. The mother hallucination, bloodstream. The crow looking at us. Here's a shape, flush with stories and figures. Something you can hold, glean, guzzle.



*Stilllife with Turbulent Water*
Collage by Zac Pranji

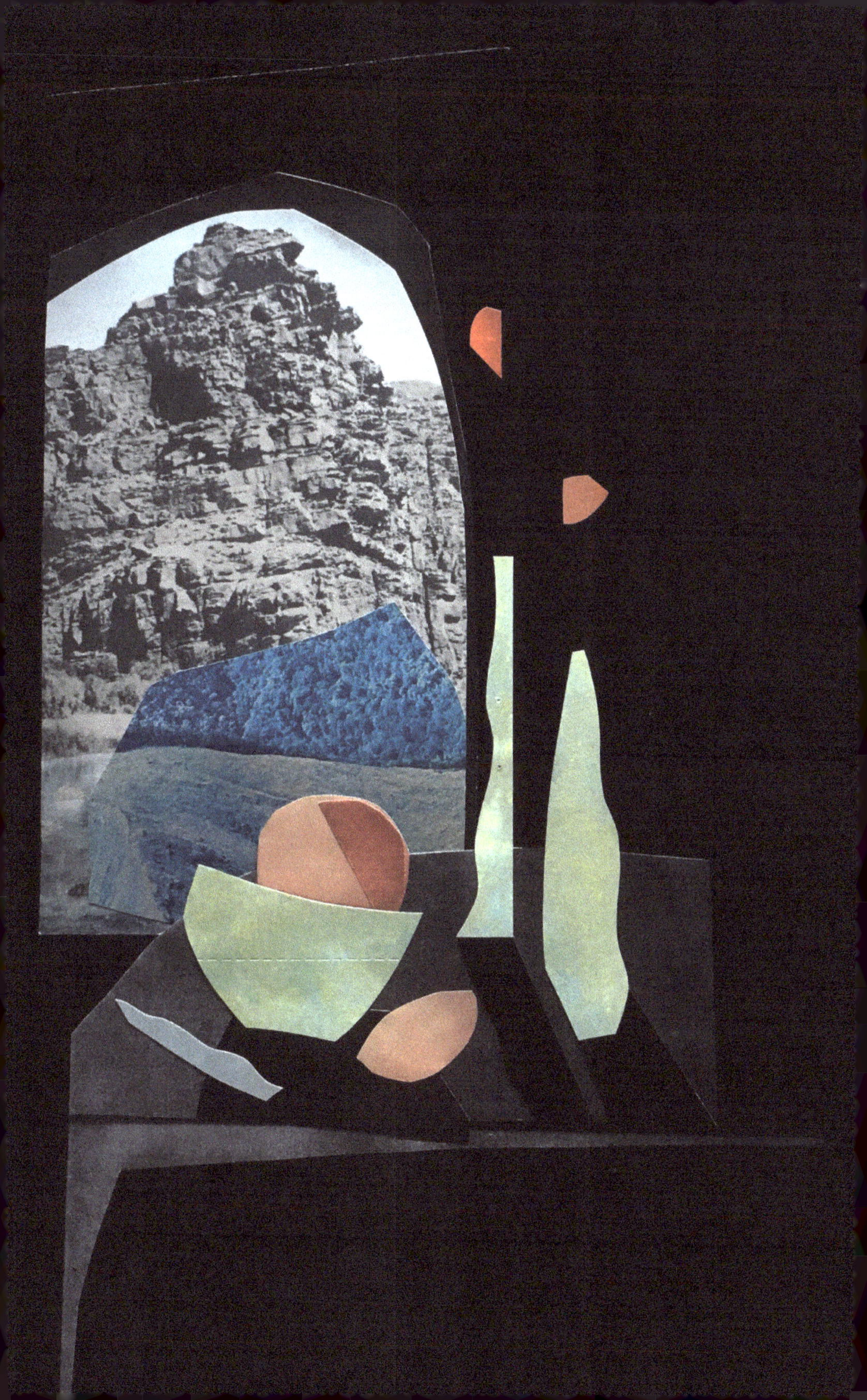

# About the
# COVER

With this cover, we wanted to show the many facets of gorge—as it appears in nature, a deep expanse; the act of indulgence, up to the brim; as slang for something stunning, *so gorge!*

In that same broad-spectrum spirit, Buckman always does our best to show the fullest range of forms and their creators, which often begs questions: *what does it mean to be creative? When is something considered an art? What mediums might be overlooked by the 'fine art' world, or by print? What about the art of self-expression, of self-decoration?*

So we sought to capture the beauty of a bejeweled nature. Manicured hands draped in metals, luster, and fruit juices. The body decorated by nails and jewelry, meticulously crafted by the hands of artists. Colorful candies, gems, and florals alike, eyes feasting. But also allowing the uglier side, the ravenous cavern demanding to be filled. Too much of a good thing until it spills over, coating all those precious shimmery pieces.

The photos were shot with both film and digital by Paisley Lee, who also the did the lighting and photo editing. The nail set was created and worn by Sam Sangermano. The concept, props, fabrication, and styling was a collaborative effort between Paisley, Sam, and Team Buck. A special thank you to Garbie Studio for providing the space to shoot.

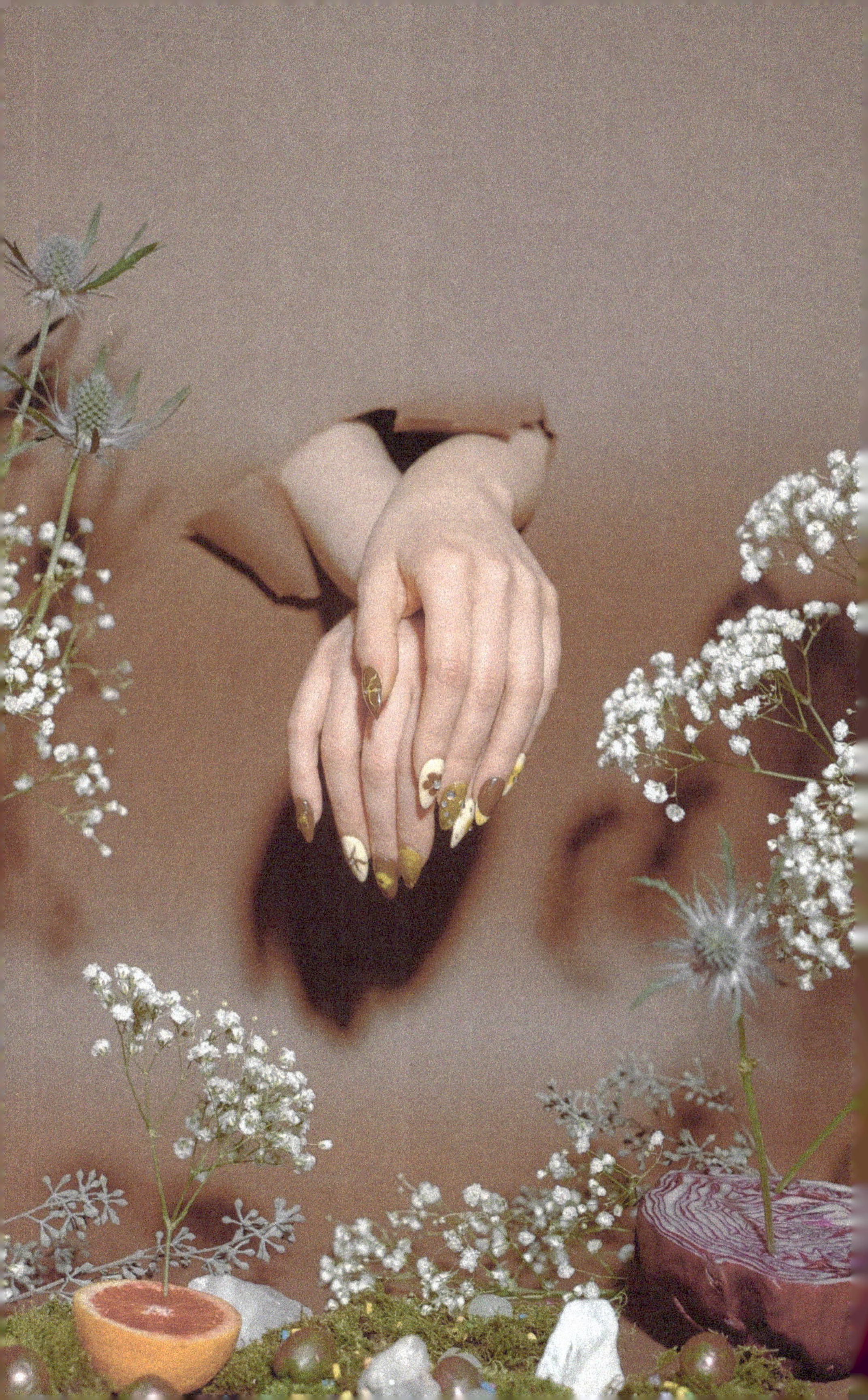

Featuring jewelry by: **Aiyana @y.eeen**
**@christinamrozikart** moth
chain ring, **Preciosa Shop by M**
beaded chain, **Snake River Jewelry**
**@taivautierjewelry** two gemstone rings,

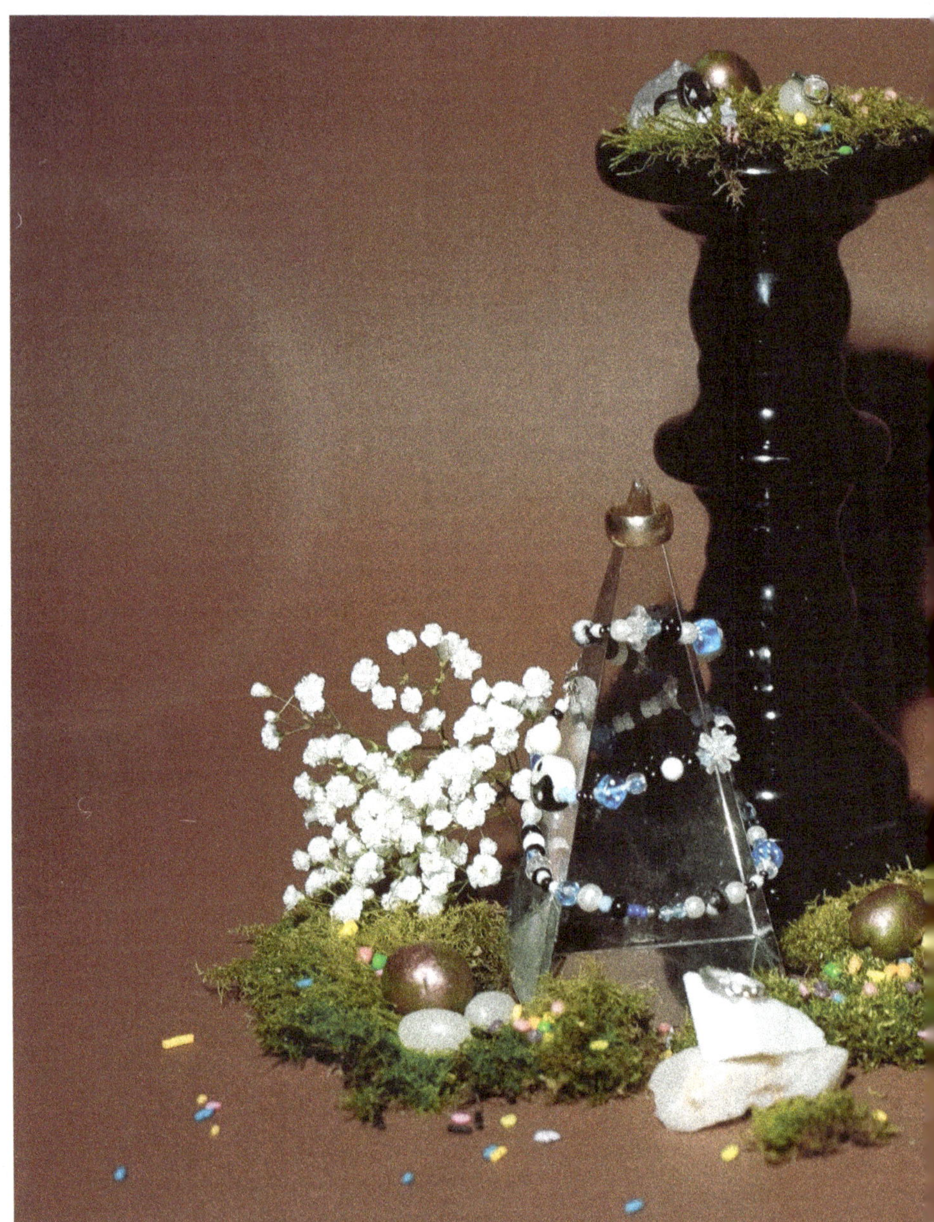

pearl necklace, **Christina Mrozik**
pin, **Gunthur @gunthurgoods**
**Gonzales @shop__preciosa**
**@snakeriver___** field ring, **Tai Vautier**
**Tiro Tiro @tirotiro** knot ring & vos ring

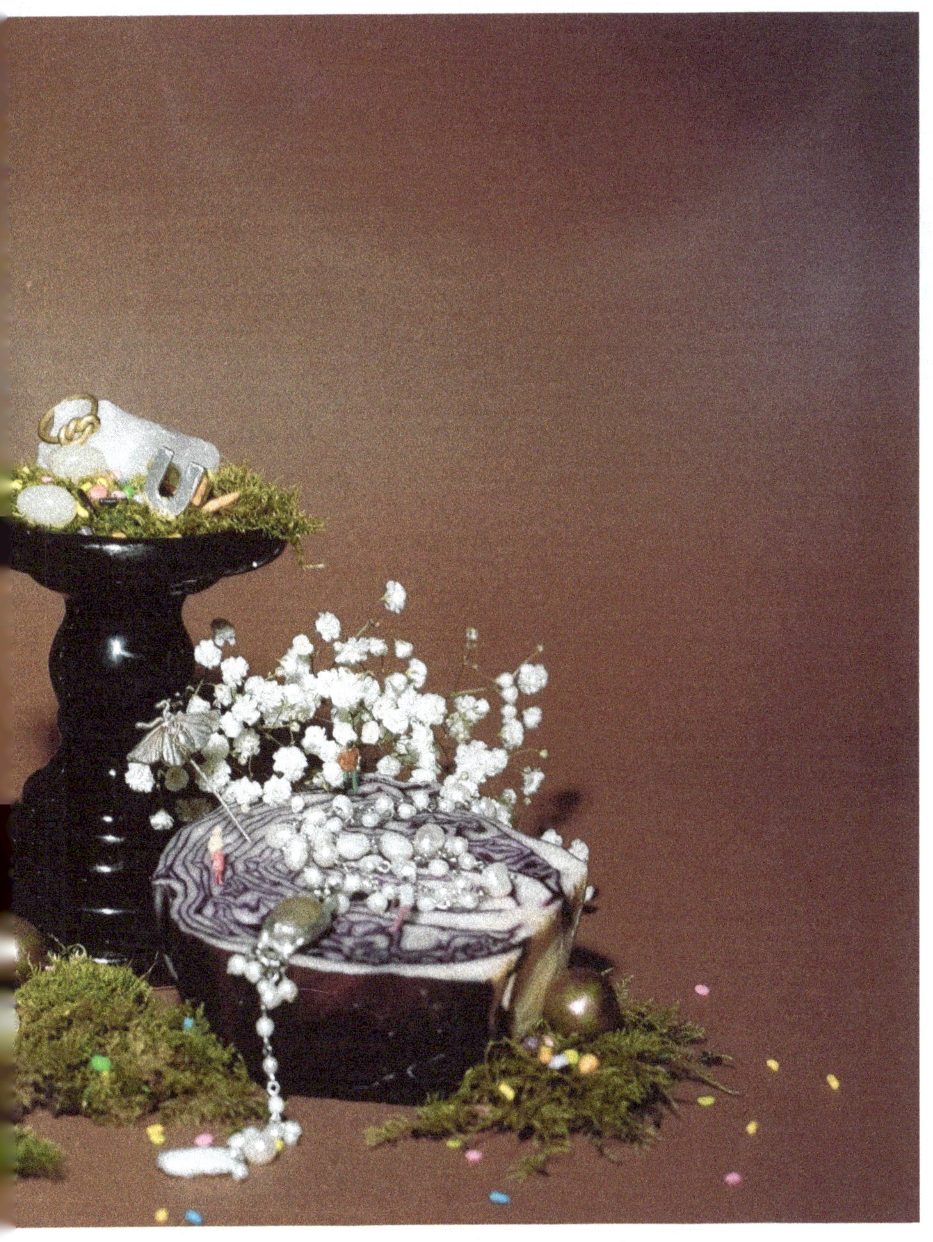

# THE

Fiction by Hannah Love

# DIVE

The bartender looks older than time itself—a face of bottomless eyes and dry canyons. His cheeks jut out in two bony cliffs, and his skin clings to them in sheets, remnants of an ancient river. He smiles, exposing gray teeth with gaps between them that seem deep enough to fall into. The stench of his breath pushes toward me. I tilt back on my heels and press my lips together. The wad of cash in my pocket feels like a stone anchoring me in place.

"Please," he says, pulling a bottle off the shelf, "sit." He knows why I came. There is only one drink sold here, and I am the only one in the bar.

I pause. Good sense and fear eddy through me, pulling me in a reverse undertow that urges me to forget all about this place. But then it's in the shot glass before me: a swirling shadowy thing that looks more like vapor than liquid.

I stare at my feet and drag my eyes across the carpet and up the walls. Everything is wrapped in deep purple galaxies—the whole bar a fabric of fading planets orbiting around us. My hands shake as I trace a velvet moon on top of the stool below me. It's so dark here I can hardly tell where my fingers end and the crescent begins.

Before all this, I would normally go to Houlihan's when I'm low because Houlihan's is sunny and familiar. I like to bask in the warm oranges and reds of the walls. I like to sit in the soft glow of the ceiling lamps and the playful silhouettes they cast along the bar top. I watch the shadows dance, I drink, I let memories fizz over my tongue: Happy, drunken birthdays. My engagement. A new job. Keys to a fancy apartment. A parking ticket tucked under my windshield wiper, dog shit caked to the bottom of my last good pair of boots.

It's strange that I learned about this darker place there, in my usual boozy refuge, but then again, darkness had been seeking me out, crawling out of corners, spreading over the edges like spilled ink. It was a rainy night in a stormy week, and there I was, slamming beers with Tommy, sucking down amber ale like it was my religion. As if by consuming enough of it, I could lure the light out of me again, draw it up from whatever hole it had fallen into.

"I'm gonna get evicted," I say, picking up my drink and glugging it fast.

"Tough luck, man," he replies, belching.

I grimace and turn toward him. He's not even looking at me. His eyes are fixed on his drink. I watch him lift it to his lips. His thick throat bobs as he swallows. He empties the glass, then sets it down and asks for another. I look around the tavern. Everyone else is doing the same thing. No one is even talking. The beer sours on my tongue, but I keep drinking.

I finish my pint and plant my elbows on the edge of the bar, pressing my palms against my temples. My vision lands on the filthy floor: discarded peanut shells, smears of gum, puddles of drying alcohol. It's all a spinning mess miles below me. Something white and blurry appears, tugging my gaze back up to the counter. It's a business card, embossed with a black circle and a phone number in skinny gray font. I run my fingers along the surface, letting them linger. Joe, the bartender, brings me a fresh beer.

"There's a place over in Buckman. For people like you," he says as he sets the glass down and taps the card. "It's a dive, but it's the real deal."

"Excuse me?" The alcohol is rising in my throat. I swallow and shove the card back across the bar. "Mind your fucking business."

"There's a drink," he continues as he slides it to me. "Changes people. Circumstances. Expensive. Worth it for some."

Heat erupts from my cheeks.

"The fuck you think you are?" I say.

The barstool topples as I get up and slam a ten-dollar bill between us. I leave the beer untouched but pocket the card. I feel it there, flat against my thigh as I stumble home.

For days, I pace around my apartment. I dial the first few digits to the place in Buckman and then hang up. My fingers finally execute the call six weeks later. The appointment is set.

The old man coughs—a rattle echoes through the bar, gravel scattering down a cliff.

I look at him, say my name, and he points to a sign. *No refunds.* I pull the cash from my pocket and start to slide it to him slowly, but he lurches forward and digs his long fingernails into the roll, clawing it the rest of the way across the bar. The silence between us deepens as he begins to count.

My mouth dries. Tommy bought me a round at Houlihan's before this, but I'm not drunk enough for what comes next. In fact, I'm not sure I've ever been prepared for anything in my entire life. The stale beer churns. I feel the urge to vomit.

"Bathroom?" I mumble.

The old man doesn't look up from the stack of cash, just shoos me away with one hand and continues counting.

Everything spins as I rush to the far corner of the bar, where I hope the bathroom is. I reach a solid black door and push my way into a stuffy one-seater. I hurtle toward the stall, drop to my knees in front of a filthy toilet. Stinking, gray water swirls beneath me. As the vomit surges, I wish I were somewhere else. Hell, I wish I were *someone* else. Someone who hadn't just spent their last dime on a rumor. Someone who didn't fall for tall tales and snake oil and sunk-cost scams. Someone who didn't believe a drink could solve his problems. I grip the edge of the seat with both hands, trying to hold myself steady through the heaves. When I'm done, I spit and tilt my head to the side. My eyes graze across something scrawled on the side of the stall in blue ink:

I SWALLOW
A BLACK HOLE
LIKE A SHOT OF TEQUILA
IN THE NAME OF SINGULARITY,
A TOAST TO INFINITE VALUE!

SWEET SHADOW
    STREAK
       THROUGH MY BODY
       MAKE ME SOMETHING
       I'M NOT

YOURS
SAPID AND STRONG
I COULD STRETCH AND
          BEND

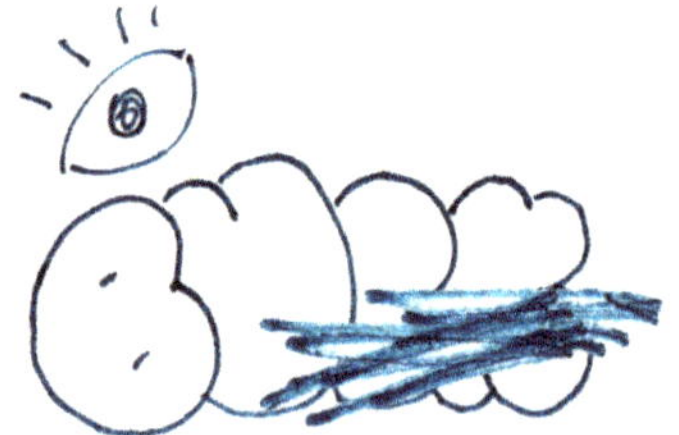

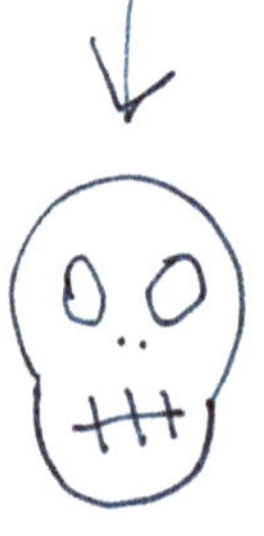

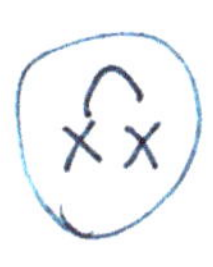

I spit into the toilet again, harder this time, and put one hand on the stall. The poem pulses beneath me. I press myself up to my feet.

My knees feel shaky and weak, but my body carries me back to the bar. I nod to the old man, but he stares straight ahead, unmoving. My drink is still there. I sit down and pick up the glass. It feels so ordinary in my hand. Cool, solid—like any other shooter from any other dive—but when I look inside, I can't see the bottom. Wispy black tendrils creep over the lip, licking at my fingers. I imagine taking a sip: my throat bursting into flames, my organs popping like water balloons. I'm not ready to die. I lift the drink higher, tipping it slightly, and the shadow slants toward me. I shut my eyes.

# BEACH

Excerpt from an in-progress novel
by S. Z. James

# HOUSE

Photography by John Kirkley

Saturday morning I sat up in my bed, surprisingly clear-headed, and looked at my grandfather's watch. It was one of those rare pure moments when everything in life comes into focus, and you can take the whole thing and turn it into an object to be manipulated and pored over, looking for any cracks or mistakes in the fabrication.

When the original pitch came the night before, all of us were sitting on Oliver's floor, the rain pouring across the windows and the whole scene lit by amber lamps and flickering fire. I had been so comfortable and intoxicated that I had forgotten I originally came here to lose myself. Of course, I had been unconsciously doing it the whole time, not realizing what I was doing by burying myself in this new life. I had moved in with a girl I only just met. I was going out every weekend and putting whatever powder someone proffered up my nose or on my tongue. What else could all that be called but running? Now I felt I had blown past the finish line and kept going, skipping the awards ceremony and the free water and donuts and hauling on until I no longer even knew the route and the trail disappeared.

I didn't want to abandon my new friends, of course. They helped me a great deal in the past year. I felt as if I belonged with them. Sometimes, when we were all lying in various states of decomposition, and I got to talking, and one of them opened up, I learned that we had all been drawn together to this point in our lives like iron filings to a magnet. All of them, without exception, had some secret, some trauma deep down that they carried with them, that disaffected them from the straight and narrow. We were all trying to lose ourselves, throw ourselves from a cliff into this hedonism. I came to this conclusion months before, but without anywhere to go, it could only roil inside me, building up pressure. The most I could do was blow off steam. What Oliver did for me was give me a pursuit, a goal. A raison d'être. I wanted his plan to work. It seemed so perfect in that crystal moment that I felt tears spring to my eyes. If there was anywhere that I could go to forget about everything, it was surely there, that imaginary place that Oliver conjured last night.

Oliver could be fickle, though. Maybe he'd just been rambling, hadn't been serious. None of the others seemed as interested. Maybe I was now the one carrying the torch, Oliver the relay runner who, without realizing it, passed me the burning idea and said *here you go, figure it out.* I needed to talk to him. My watch read just before nine o'clock, three hours before I usually woke up, and forever until Jodie stirred herself. Oliver was sometimes an early riser, despite his habit of staying up late—he'd mentioned it one time when I asked about his eyes. He said they were a side effect of extended sleep deprivation. I knew a little bit about that, though since I'd moved into this apartment, I had forgotten my past brushes with insomnia. During those times, late at night, nobody else in the house awake, I'd wander the town. I spent hours as the only patron at the all-night diner, only Kenny the line cook for company, or driving the truck out on the back roads in the utter darkness of the West Cascades, the Milky Way peering dispassionately down on my hood through the overstory.

Insomnia had changed me, and perhaps it had changed Oliver too. Maybe that was part of the reason I'd been so

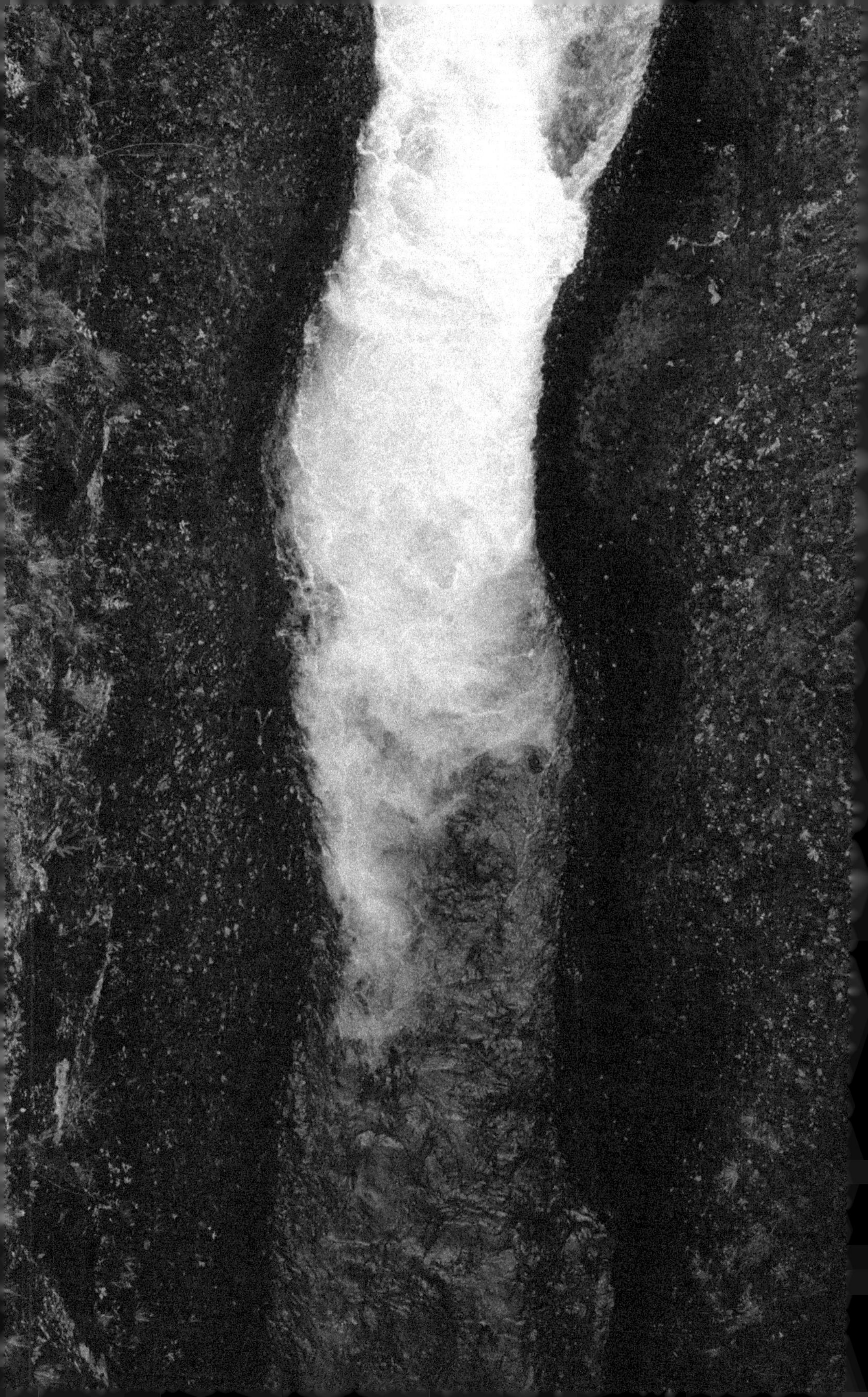

drawn to him at first; an addict recognizing a fellow twelve-stepper. Likely he was awake now. I showered and dressed and had the phone ringing in my hand before I realized I didn't have the question ready.

"Hello?" Came the voice down the line.

"Hey, Oliver, it's Ocean."

"Guten morgen, Ocean. How can I be of service?"

"I wanted to talk about the commune thing…"

"What?"

"The thing you were talking about last night. With the property on the coast range and the subsidized farming and stuff."

"Oh, shit! Yeah, I forgot about that. What was the question again?"

I paused, a bit crestfallen. Fickle indeed.

"Uh, I guess I just wanted to say I really liked the idea." This was coming out strange.

"Thanks, man. Yeah, it would definitely be cool, but I don't know if we can convince everybody. Obviously, it'd be great if everyone was on board, and if we could have like twenty people that'd be sick, but I think it'd end up being just you and me and maybe Sean."

Twenty people? "How much have you thought this through?"

"Tell you what, Ocean, old sport." I could hear his smirk. "Why don't you meet me at Coffee Time? I'll tell you the whole thing."

"Where's that?"

"21st and Irving, next to the movie theater."

Coffee Time turned out to be a dark hole-in-the-wall serving pastries and breakfast sandwiches. It seemed like a very good place to nurse a hangover, which Oliver no doubt was, considering he was wearing his sunglasses when I sat down next to him. He acknowledged me with a raise of his coffee mug.

"You sounded very mysterious over the phone."

"Yes. This is now a plot. You are an accomplice to conspiracy."

"Are we kidnapping people?" I took a delicate sip to test the temperature of my latte and got scalded.

"Not really, just convincing them to leave their comfortable apartments and regular bars and favorite restaurants to come live in the middle of nowhere."

"And how do you propose we do that?"

Oliver leaned back in his chair with a heavy sigh. He sometimes moved like a man three times his age, as if his joints were weary from a life spent in hard labor. This, combined with his habit of wearing suit jackets, made him seem like an old man trapped in a young man's body. He peered through his sunglasses at the light filtering through the paneled windows.

"I don't know. Like I said, it's just an idea. I thought maybe we'd try to win them over until we have a majority."

"Sounds kind of manipulative."

"Yeah."

We sat in silence for a while, sipping our drinks and trying to force our fogged-up minds through the wall of problems. My accomplice was not as passionate as I had hoped, which was a bit dampening, but I was still determined.

It came to me all at once, out of the corner of my vision, where it had been all along. It was stupid, and irresponsible, and would no doubt raise questions. I shouldn't even have thought of it in the first place; but in the heat of the moment, I couldn't resist.

"Shit!" I said, perhaps a bit too loud; we drew stares.

"What?"

I had to tell him. If I didn't, I would regret it, I was sure. So I did the thing I wasn't supposed to do, that I shouldn't have done.

"Remember how my aunt's house burned down?"

He nodded. "What does that have to

do with anything?"

"Well I didn't say this before cause it's kinda weird, but a few months after the fire a guy with the insurance company showed up and he gave me some money." Oliver's sunglasses caught a glare and blazed for a moment with daylight fire.

"How much money?"

"A lot." I trusted Oliver, to an extent, but I'd never told anyone about the insurance payout before, and I wasn't about to divulge everything.

"Enough for a plot of land in the coast range?"

"Maybe. Do you think if we tell people they wouldn't have to pay for the land, we could do it?"

# I would realize my foolish ways and abandon my new life here for a more familiar one.

Now that it was real, the possibility of actually moving to the middle of nowhere scared me more than I thought it would. Suddenly I was more hesitant to leave behind my nice, comfortable life in the city with Jodie. But wasn't this what I planned to do the whole time?

"I think there's a very real possibility. Are you sure you want to spend your money like this?"

"On oceanfront property? Are you kidding me? What's the worst that could happen?" *A tsunami, an earthquake, a flood, a fire…*

Oliver was galvanized. The money had clearly been the biggest roadblock for him; he had no qualms about the action itself. His hangover cured by ambition, he stood up and removed his sunglasses. His eyes were steady on mine.

"Okay. I'm going to figure out exactly how much money we need. I'll call you when I find out." He turned to leave, and then added: "Don't tell anybody yet, I want it to be a surprise."

His determination was both heartening and intimidating. I hadn't seen this side of him before; the Oliver that would actually work hard to get something he wanted. I was used to him lounging in his armchair, surrounded by partygoers, in the manner of a king holding court; aloof and subdued. As though he were surveying the landscape and, though it pleased him, to show as much on his face would be beneath him. This other Oliver was less a monarch than an explorer, earnest and intrepid. It was strange, to see on someone else's face how I thought I'd felt until I'd revealed my inheritance, which was how I'd started to think of it. If my aunt's will remained sealed because she was missing, not dead, then I could treat the insurance money as though it were mine by birthright. The cops had stopped looking for her. They'd told me a year before I graduated high school. The lawyer who called when I turned eighteen told me she couldn't be presumed dead until she'd been missing for seven years. *In the meantime, would you like to look over some documents? We'd like to begin the process of selling her house.*

I declined to sign away the house, though it would have meant more money in my pocket. There was still some part of me that believed she would show up one day at the front door, and she would be incensed if I had sold it off. Besides, the place was basically my childhood home. I couldn't in good conscience let it go just because my aunt had left. So I paid the annual bills, the landscapers who came once a season, the plumber I called

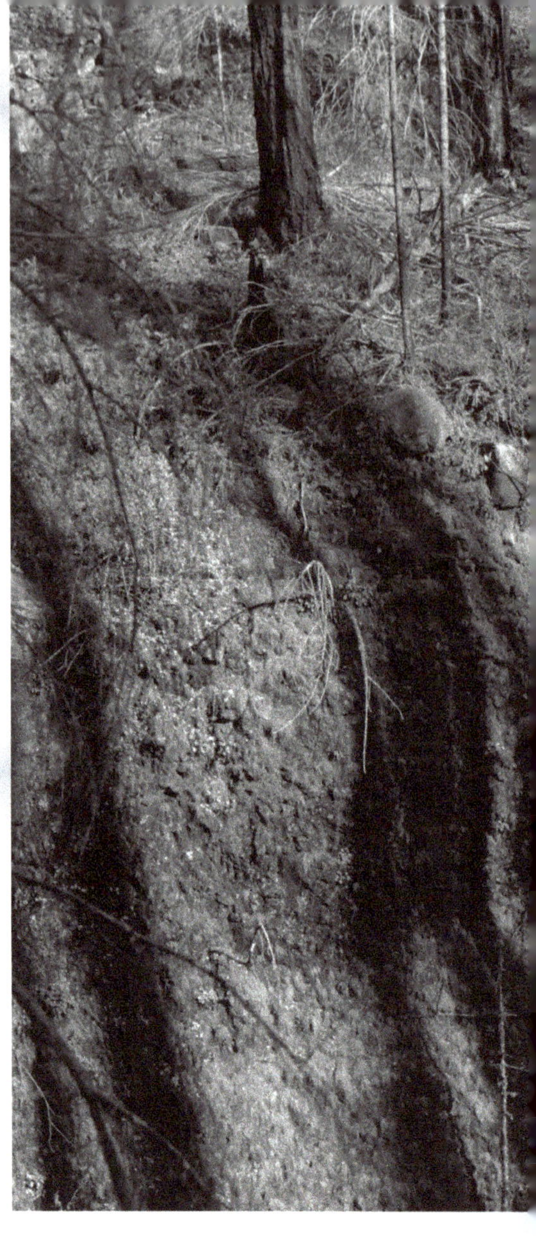

when the septic tank sprung a leak for no reason last July, and over the phone I supplicated myself to the lawyer, Mr. Gary E. Schwartz, to look after the place. To him this probably meant passing by once a month or so to make sure it hadn't fallen down. I worried about it sometimes; were raccoons infesting the basement, termites destroying the old beams that held the place up? But even with all my worrying I hadn't been back to Witches to check on it. I felt that if I returned to that place, that enclave, I would realize my foolish ways and abandon my new life here for a more familiar one.

I sat alone in the coffee shop for some time, nursing my latte and watching people pass by on the sidewalk. There was a sense of calmness before the storm, of perching on the brink. I had already uprooted my life once before, and though it had been a bit terrifying, everything turned out alright. There was still that gnawing feeling of discontent in

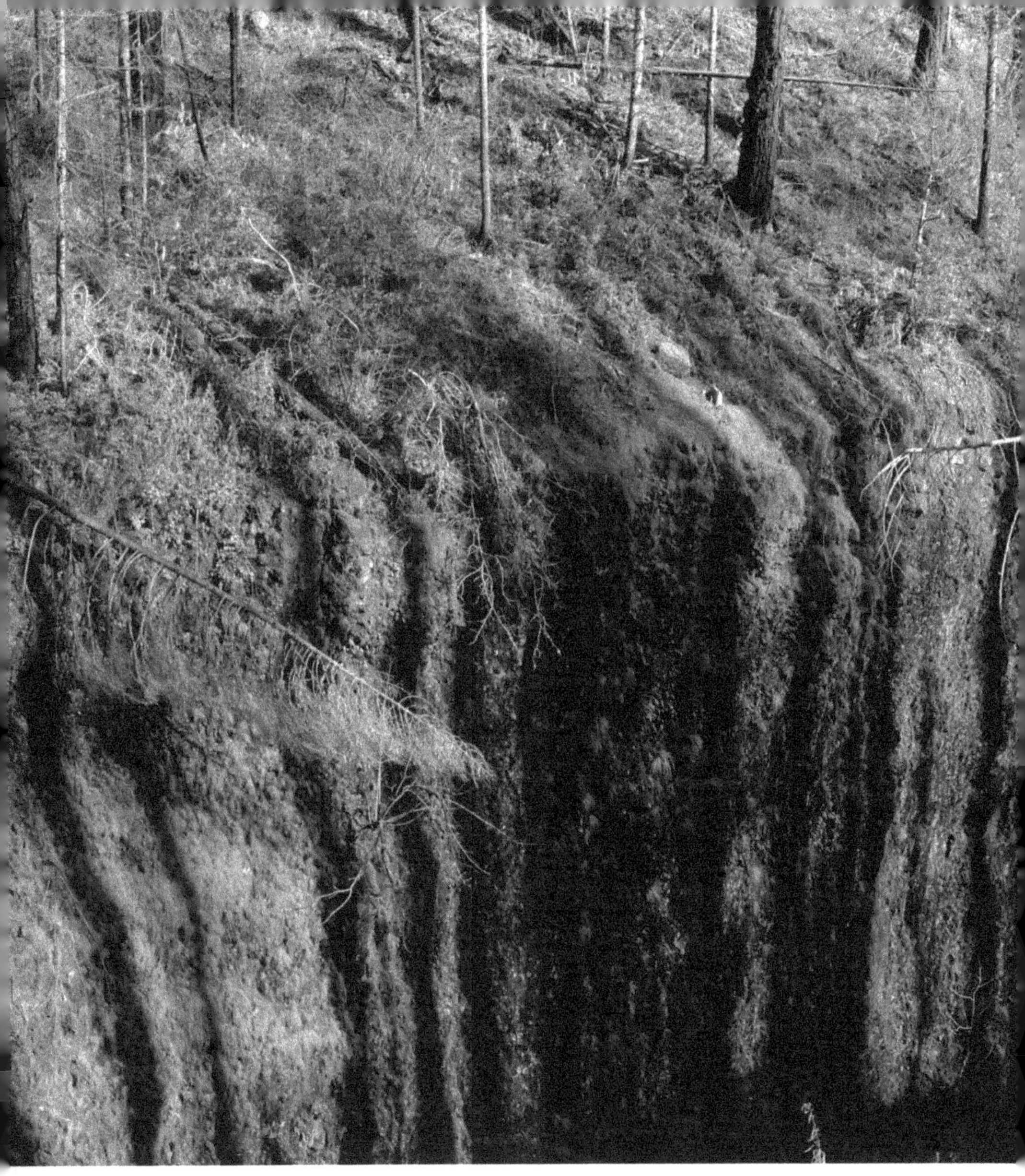

my guts, that I'd thought was gone for a while but had returned, slowly at first, and then ravenously, a hungry parasite.

It wasn't just that I needed to get far away from my hometown, it was that I needed to get far away from everything. The fire still chased me; in dreams, I would smell smoke, but never see flames, and bolt upright in bed, sweating and terrified. I was beginning to think it was something that would follow me for the rest of my life, chasing me through the dark corridors of my aunt's house, unless I did something about it. I already developed escape plans for Jodie's and Oliver's apartments, and sat down with Jodie to go over exactly what to do in the event of a fire in various places in the building. But how does one fight a dream fire? There was nothing I could do when it came for me in the night. My insomnia may have abated, but in its place came the dreams, and I was helpless in their grasp.

My eyes glazed over in the coffee shop. Curling, licking flames danced behind them, and my thoughts blackened to soot before I snapped out of it. The only thing to do was keep running. I could run forever from this, and maybe in time it would get tired and stop chasing me.

A week later, Oliver called me. He said he'd found someone who had some property for sale outside Neskowin, which I'd never heard of. Listening to him describe it, it was a paradise. "Huge beach, nobody around. Total privacy! Just us and the sea." The land was a parcel of five acres, with an old house and a few outbuildings that Oliver thought were probably in desperate need of resuscitation, but which the realtor had espoused as being "rustic," whatever that was supposed to mean. We were to go out and take a look at it this Tuesday.

"Should we tell everyone else? Jodie and Sean probably want to come look at it."

"Maybe. Not yet, probably we should wait until we know if it's even any good." He looked absolutely thrilled. I'd never seen him with so much energy. His transformation had taken a serious hold. He had done nothing but plan the trip and the inevitable completion of 'our little project,' as he called it. "She said it's going for thirty-five. That's fifteen below budget!"

He looked so excited that I felt bad shooting him down; the "budget" he was talking about was my personal fortune. "Let's at least wait until we see it to decide anything. For all we know it could just be a bunch of rotting planks."

Still, his enthusiasm was infectious. Who else was it at the party who had seemed like they might actually want to go through with it? Sean, maybe, though he had been so drunk I wasn't sure he remembered anything about the conversation at all. Alice had been concerned about it being a cult, so she was likely out. Jodie was always down for anything, but I wanted to surprise her; plus, she was the only one of us who had anything resembling a real job. Oliver had the affectations of wealth, but none of the affluence. He bought furniture at garage sales, and he didn't have to pay rent because his landlord was his second cousin or something. I never found out what the others did for money. Perhaps they were like me and simply didn't have to worry about it.

Eventually, Tuesday rolled around, and I brought the truck around to Oliver's apartment and we headed west for the coast. It rained almost the whole way. There was a brief respite as we crested the coast range and the sun came out, shining on my beat-up pickup through the canopy above. The ever-present sentinels of the rainforest, sluiced by asphalt. We didn't talk much on the drive over, except about the property and how excited we were by it. Clara, the real estate agent, hadn't sent any pictures over. I was envisioning a clearing bordered by gnarled pine trees, gray from the wind and rain, an old driftwood bungalow, and a view of the ocean in the background, like a painting in a vacation home's nautical-themed bathroom.

The driveway had once been clear and wide, and visible from the road, but in order to find the place we had to park at the mile marker and walk until we saw the yellow *Oregonian* newspaper box hidden behind the foliage. There was a footpath that led into the property, and after much debate about whether or not this was it, and if it wasn't, whether the current occupant would chase us off the property with a shotgun, we ventured into the bracken. The path was long and winding, and took us over a prefabricated steel bridge that looked wide enough for a car, over a creek, and into a clearing. Surprisingly, I was not let down, though it wasn't exactly the way I'd pictured it. In the middle of the patch of open ground sat the bungalow, a ramshackle thing that looked like it was about one soft push from falling down, but at least it still had a roof. The lights were on, another pleasant surprise, and there was a figure sitting on the porch: Clara. She was bundled up against the November chill in a businesslike topcoat and scarf, and as we emerged from the forest path, she stood up to greet us. I didn't see any of the outbuildings; they must have been hidden by the encroaching trees.

Clara didn't seem at all surprised that we were as young as we were. She stepped off the porch. She was the image of a professional: clad in a gray suit beneath her coat, hair in a tight ponytail, makeup subtle and clean. She would have been entirely unremarkable were it not for her fingernails: they were two inches long, bright red, and came to points that looked as though they would hurt to get stabbed by. She approached us with confident, long strides.

"Oliver!" Her voice did not match her appearance at all. She sounded as if she'd been smoking since the womb. Oliver's face cracked in a grin.

"Clara, darling. Hello again." They exchanged a European greeting, kisses on both sides of the mouth, and I wondered exactly how these two knew each other.

"And who are you?" She asked, turning to me.

"Ocean. Pleased to meet you."

"Likewise." Clapping her hands and rubbing them together, she turned back to the house. "I'm glad you boys are here. We've had a real hard time selling this place." Now that she mentioned it, why was a real estate agent from Portland representing a property all the way out here? I asked her as much, and she gave a slight smile and said "Oh, we have numerous properties throughout the state. Half of the job is just driving to get to them all!" She laughed, which would have sounded insincere from someone

else, but from her, it somehow seemed genuine. She reminded me of a farmer I had known in Witches, who would sometimes come into the diner late at night and talk cheerfully to the waitresses, all of whom seemed to adore him. Salt of the earth, they called him.

"So this is the main building. Built sometime last century, we're not sure exactly when, and it was abandoned several years ago, as you can see, but it's still in decent shape." To demonstrate this, or perhaps just for effect, she knocked on one of the walls. She was in full sales mode. "Shall we go inside?"

We assented. The door creaked open like it hadn't seen use since the house was built. Inside it was pleasantly quaint. A woodstove stood in the middle of what seemed to be the main room with doorways into a small kitchen on one side and a bedroom without a bed on the other. The walls were papered with grasscloth, showing through in places to older patterns. The floor seemed to be original to the building; dark, wide planks smoothed by age. It smelled of mothballs and lemon-scented wood cleaner. They must have tried to shine the place up for our visit. "It's a one-bedroom, as you can see, with an attached bathroom. Excellent views of the coastline and the surrounding forest, as you can see." She opened a plaid curtain that looked to be from the midcentury. "This is a special case, as we don't know the original owner, but we think it was originally either a vacation home or a hunting lodge. As you can see, some of the decor"—she pointed to a ten-point elk antler trophy hung high on one wall—"supports the hunting lodge theory." Our host seemed to say "as you can see" a lot. I wandered off by myself as Oliver tailed our guide, asking the occasional question as to the provenance of the decorations, the wallpaper, the woodstove. He looked about the room with the eye of a trained appraiser.

I peeked into the bathroom, which

was surprisingly ornate: clawfoot tub big enough for two moderately-sized occupants, hexagonal tiling on the floors and countertops. The overall impression of the place was of something that had been well-loved once but had since fallen into disrepair. I was reminded of *The Giving Tree*, one of my favorites that my aunt used to read to me when I was very small. I felt a strange protective urge toward this place. The house, so settled, was familiar in the way old places sometimes are, rife with the weight of time, the sense that people had made lives here before, and would do so again.

I left the bathroom and perused the main room, brushing the grasscloth with one finger; then to the kitchen. I opened a few cupboards because I felt like that was what you were supposed to do when looking at a property. Nothing out of the ordinary. Oliver and Clara were standing out on the porch, and I joined them. Clara was pointing off into the woods.

"Past those trees. Do you see it? It's a little hard to make out."

Oliver stepped to the edge of the porch, craning his neck. "I think so? Is it that black lump?"

Clara nodded. "That's one of them, yeah." I followed Oliver's gaze. There was something behind the trees, though I couldn't make out its exact silhouette. Likely one of the outbuildings.

"Can we go look at it?" Oliver asked. He looked like a puppy begging for scraps. He was ecstatic as we traipsed through the beargrass. In his mind, this was already a done deal.

The outbuilding was a low structure. What might once have been an icehouse was now renovated into a livable room with a stone floor and wood-paneled walls. It looked to be about ten feet by ten feet, big enough for a bed and a desk, maybe.

"It's older than the house, originally, at least we think so." Clara stepped into the space. "There was presumably another building on the lot at some point, possibly in the nineteenth century, but it's gone now. These dugouts are all that's left of them, and as you can see, the previous owner turned them into these little guest rooms. Aren't they nice?" She gestured toward the walls. "They even added windows. "They didn't seem all that nice to me, in fact they seemed like fancy cells, but Oliver liked them, and he said as much.



Some more trailing behind Clara and trying to figure out what to do with my hands, and we returned to the car. Clara had parked around the corner, she said, but did we have any last questions?

"Yes, actually. You said the figure was thirty-five?" Oliver asked.

Clara nodded. "Thirty-five fifty." After a pause and an inquisitive glance, she waved and walked away. I heard the click of her cigarette lighter as she vanished behind the trees.

Oliver turned to me, a widening of his mouth making it obvious he'd already made up his mind. "Isn't it perfect?" He said as we got in the truck. "It has a view, the house is nice, and it has room for ten people. Clara said there were a bunch more of those dugouts around."

30

He spoke fast, the same cadence as when he'd first pitched the idea on the floor of his living room. "And it's fifteen thousand under budget? It's perfect!" He said again, "And it isn't too far from town! We'd be able to set up shop there no problem. Now we just have to convince everyone to come out here, and we'll be set. Right?" He looked me in the eyes, waiting for a reply. I met his gaze, then looked at the road. "Right." He could sense my shift in attitude and kept pressing his case. I wasn't sure about it. "It's a lot of money, sure, but like you said, how bad could it be? An oceanfront property? It's only going to get more valuable. You know how many Californians are buying property on the coast right now?" The gravel road shook the car. We were losing the light; the sun was slowly sinking into the ocean on our left side. It lit up the sky, and the orange and pink blended to rose and shone through Oliver's hair. It gave him an almost heavenly appearance, that old trope, the angel on my shoulder. And besides, he was right. I wasn't being stupid, I was being smart. And this was exactly what I'd hoped for.

"Yeah, I know. You're right." He leaned back in his seat, victorious. "Now what do we say to everyone to convince them?"

"Don't worry about that, old sport," he said, confidence brimming in his voice, as the sun slipped under the gray-blue water in the distance. "They're more open-minded than you think." He reached to turn up the stereo, and the harmonies of The Hollies CD Jodie burned for me soothed my worries. I forgot all about the huge sum of money I was about to spend. The tree-lined highway twisted and gleamed and spit us out back in Portland two hours later.

As it turned out, Oliver was right. To this day I don't know how he did it, or so quickly, but he convinced almost everyone to come along. Probably got them all liquored up and then gave a big speech. There were a few holdouts, Molly among them, but Oliver said they'd change their minds as soon as the rest of us made the move. I was given the task of convincing Jodie, which turned out to be easier than I'd expected.

"Honestly, that sounds way better than what I have going on here." We were in her bedroom, on the four-poster. The city hummed outside, but the thick curtains were closed and the heavy smell of incense hung in the air. It was dim, the only light source was the bedside lamp she had found at an estate sale in the hills, and we were drunk on a cheap bottle of wine Sean had given her for her birthday.

"Really?" I'd figured she would want to stay at her mysteriously easy high-paying job. She looked at me.

"Yeah, I mean, why not? You said it yourself, there's no rent, there's not any real stress. And besides, I hate my job. I hate having to go into an office, ever. It feels gross, and it is gross, some of those guys in there." She made a face. "I was in from the start."

This was excellent news, and I said so. Jodie smiled in a way that nearly killed me. It felt as if things were coming together, like what I had set out to do when I left Witches was finally bearing fruit; that all my life to this point had been a rehearsal, a preamble. It was finally time to begin the real thing.

I was reminded of a role-playing game I was obsessed with back in Witches. Thor got me into it. "This feels like an adventure," I said. "Like we're setting out." Her eyes in the semi-darkness looked blue-black. She shook her head, and her hair fell in front of her face. "You're such a dork," she said, and pushed me over. I kept talking, smiling now, leaning into it. "It's a quest. We've gathered the party, and now we're going on an adventure."

# ODE

# CRE

Poetry by Andrew Simon

# TO

# ASES

Sculpture by Alex Diamond

Green velour lakelands thrust to discover continental pavilions held up to hug with gas station presents engorged from butter bug dreams. Morning. Me, him, her all the way—squeeze in—right here. Toppa the bleachers. Lotsa butts. Turned over in the sixth to watch the parking lot where we were taught Yiddish funny. Drove back on swampy gravel, because he had what I would have, or always did, and never knew, or always knew, and never did. Big ones taste like dirt. You're not allergic, Mr. Hot Wheels. Besides, how would you know what dirt tastes like? I learned at the Magic Place. Magic because empty on weekends. Weekends because working on days. Where we were, for the first time, only once. Like our new house. Where the greatest threat was what's on television. Tongues flapping after Doctor Park before we picked up a telephone order and—CRASH! into a hitch. Do we need another reminder about the dress code? Smile. It's the Magic Place. Reborn with a new name: The Barnes Road Professional Campus. Next stop? Brava Centauri to learn about skin conditions and swallow rust cups on glam trays. C.R.E.A.M. That's the ticket, buster. Shawls of commercial plastic-paper layered pink cake. Are they creased now? Fuss. Yellow legal pads indicating tests locked in a black box in a sunny O.P. with a parking lot and an armed guard. Thank the G.O.D. for Medical Compliance Officers. Turns out we were allergic. Meetings. More meetings. Meetings at the A.D.B. Presidential Library. Or the Smithsonian, which must be somebody else's Magic Place. Where we took a Yamaha pill to believe the tests were safe in a black box. "Quiet Please." Cassette tape archived Morgellons grandma in a ballroom off Sunset Boulevard. Just not *our* ballroom. Late with birthday wax, yellow lights, busted cameras, and the Freedom of Information Act, which I've got a copy of here in my. Hold up. Who is being carried through security, through Air & Space, through all-raw outer space? How many weeks along? How much time? How much money? How much money matters when there is no more more than more? No relativity. No Einstein. No me. No you. Only. Hospitals. War hospitals. Where people wore soft hats. Ate in cafeterias. Collected paychecks. Got along. Where a little communism worked. Beneath feet becoming carpets. Carpets becoming dirt. Dirt becoming moon. D.R.E.A.M. That's the creases, buster.

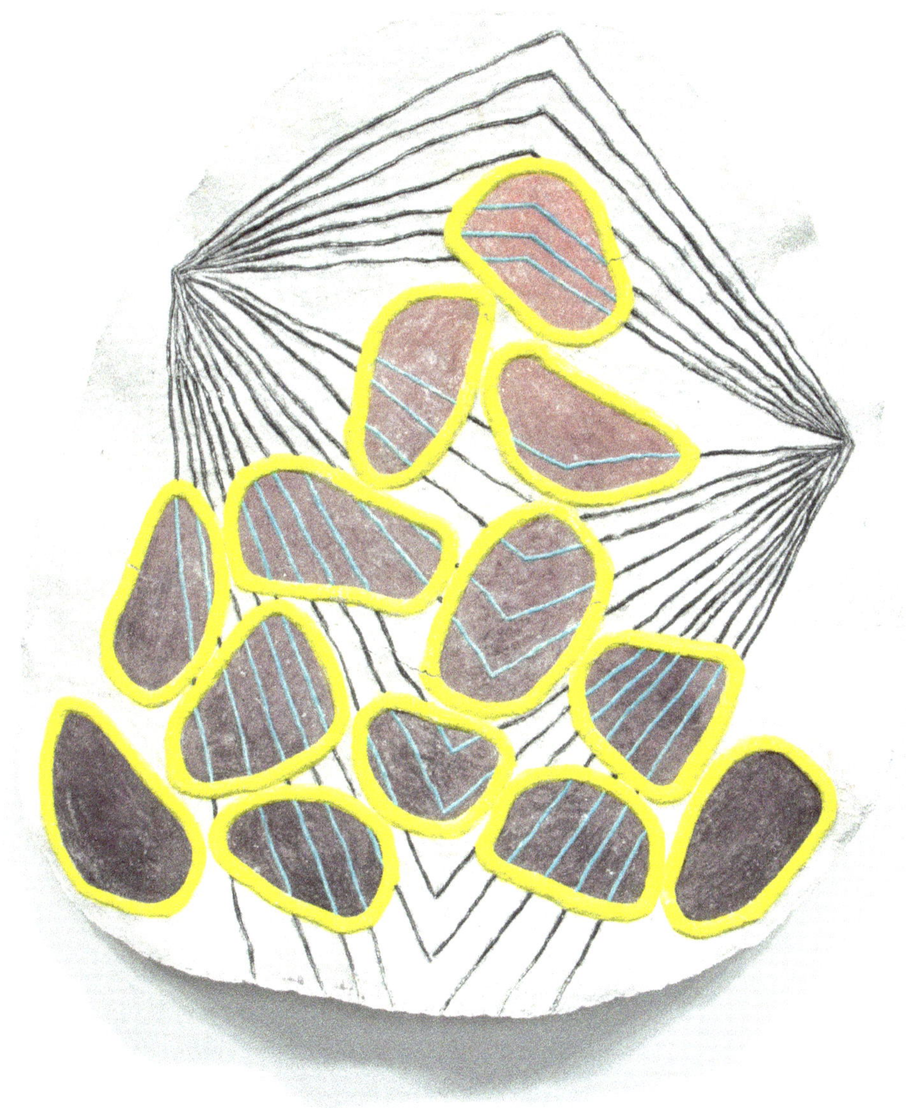

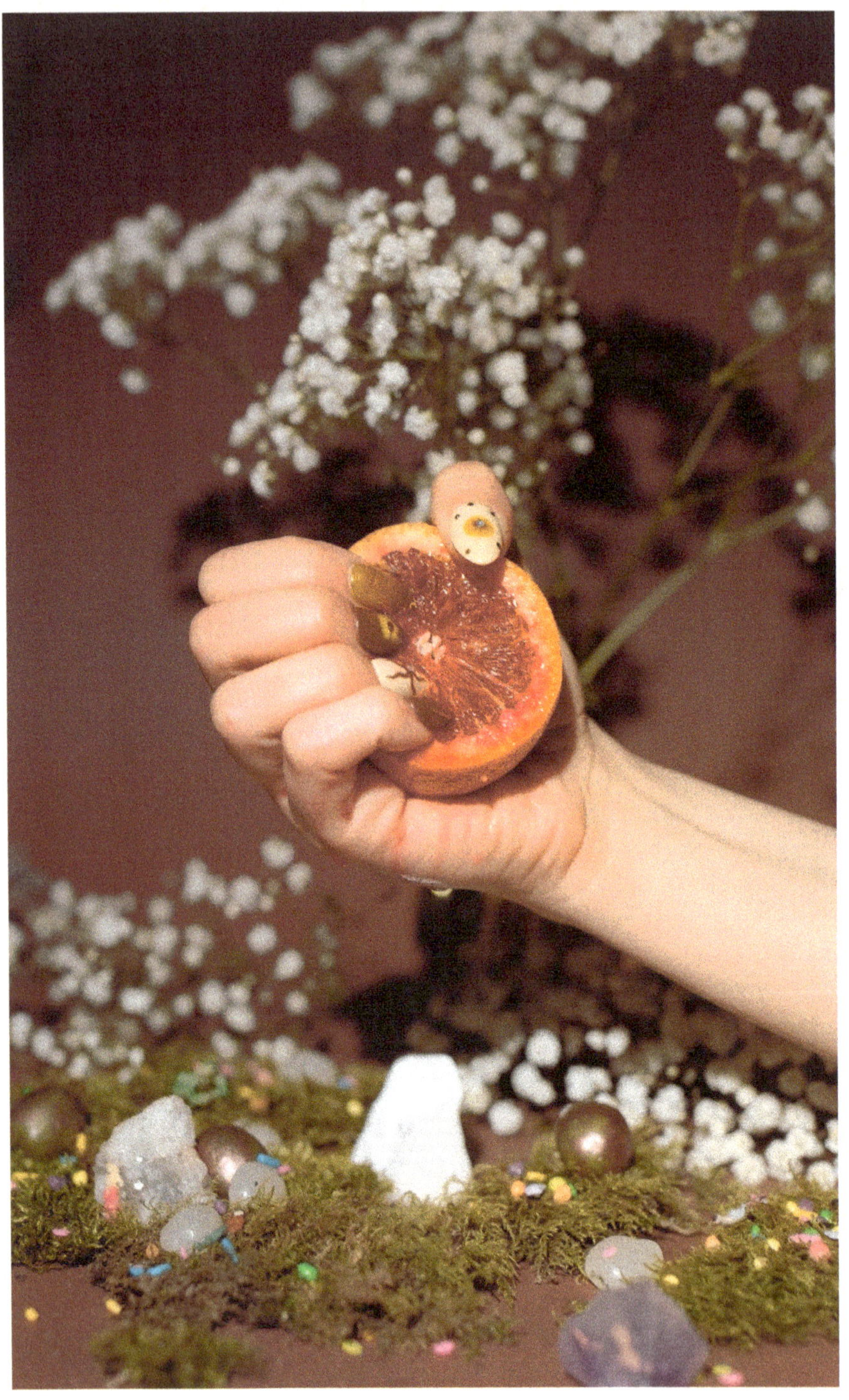

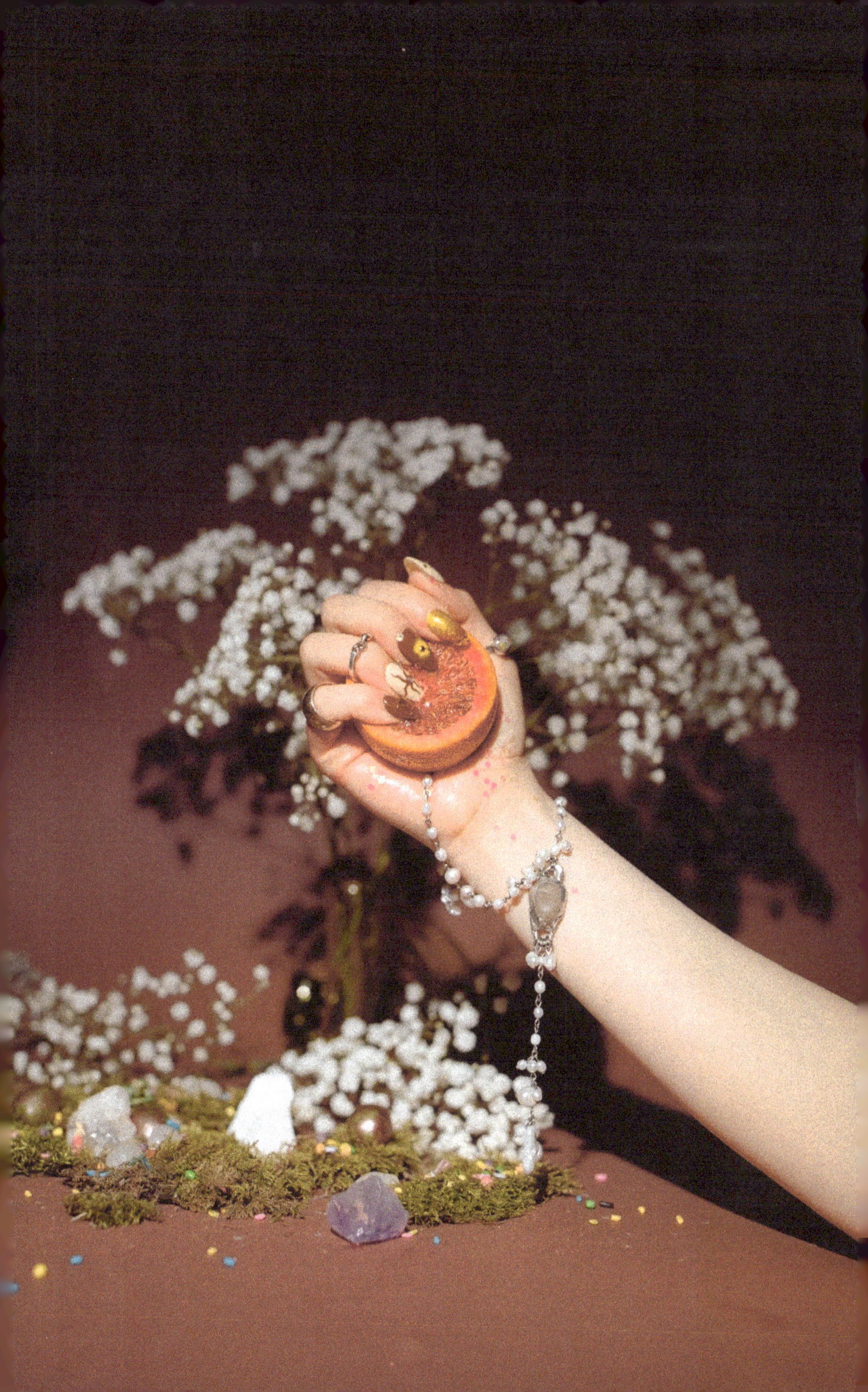

# CAR

Creative Non-Fiction by Jamie Cattanach

# VED

Drawing by Christian Johnson

I took myself back to my side of the rivers, the two I cross to get to you. Every day then, I'd wake in forgetting: which state? Which side of the chasm?

A friend told me what drew the gorge—the lake that was Missoula flooding, torrential, year after year, for millennia. For longer than we're built to understand.

The ways we move through this world, tired and soft and afraid. Bodies that slack and soften, grow gray and old regardless. The gill I sliced into my finger, small but deep, a kitchen-knife accident that stayed. The ever-present rumble of hunger—what I long called safety.

How when it happened that night—the very first time we fought—I drove home from your house in Vancouver shaking and unsure and, I found, once I stripped myself, wet.

How I found my way back to downtown Portland, rain-gray streets too loud and distant: from you, from our shared Southeastern homelands.

How distance can feel terminal—but nothing ever touches, really, at the molecular level. Not even self to self.


The entire town of Missoula was underwater, once. Was water. I went there before I knew you, while I was hungry. Afloat.

A twin-sized hostel bed in a hundred-year-old building, the river through my window. The glass warped and bubbled. The room was over a bookstore. I walked through it twice, looking. Hoping someone would look.

I was a hollowed-out bone of myself, then. I sauteed farmers-market morels in coconut oil and called it indulgence.

As the day stretched its long arms, I wandered through town: across and back. Again. The coffee shops and galleries, the bars. Looking like I was going somewhere. Looking like. Not myself.

Although the film was shot elsewhere, Missoula is the setting of *A River Runs Through It*—and one does. There's a single, manmade wave installed just beside the bridge; Brennan's wave, they call it. The boys go down in wetsuits and surf it, hovering there forever on an aquatic treadmill. Beer cans on the embankment, crushed.

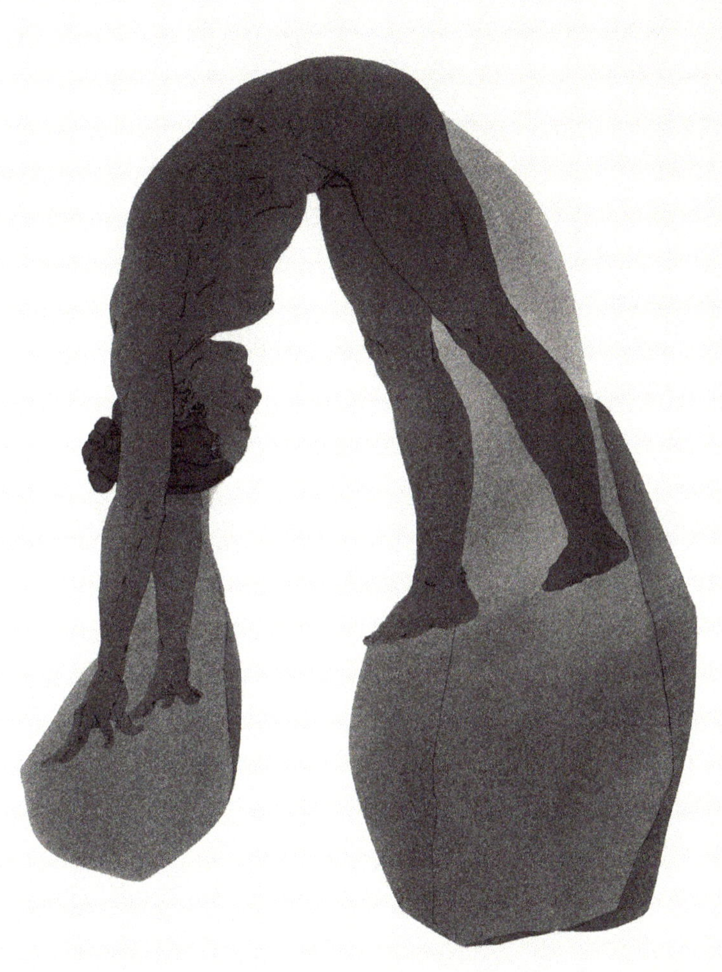

I crawled back and forth across that town, sweatless and desperate to be seen; starving. I pressed my palm to the hostel window; deposited its print. I was everywhere that year and nowhere, connected to nothing.

I'd convinced everyone—myself—that this was freedom.

A year before the rainforest, the desert. I tried, for a while, to stay.

I'd driven myself there via North Carolina and Kansas. I'd signed the lease after a day of cellphone-crying, pressed my hands against the strange-smooth bathroom counter. Could I?

*What if something happens to you?* I'd asked my mother, tear-staining someone else's couch.

*What if,* she said. *What if nothing does?*

It was Independence Day and then, the first monsoon of the season: mid-July, a not-quite apocalyptic flood. Still, cars drifted to the side of the street, emergencies blinking. Still, sideways rain under the door, the floor I'd just paid for, drenched. I drove across town to use my new key to see it: *Still life—empty house in tears.* Not still. The rain outside turned hail, turned grapefruit. The broken-backed windchimes I rescued from my neighbor's yard.

It wasn't a year later I was packing my truck. I could feel myself, inevitably, getting bigger, growing back. Terrified and humiliated, I ran. Again.

The rain was gentle, then. The man I'd been seeing came and helped me move the mattress, but only because I begged him. I'd packed the whole house in less than an afternoon.

I watched the smoke trail out of his driver's side window, following him around my corner that one last time. In the desert, you can see rain coming from so far away that it sometimes doesn't come at all. Just sits there like an omen.

A few hours from the town you were raised in, the man I gave my youth to ripped off my clothes. We were pressed against the glass of a high-rise hotel room. The city spread out below us, potent and sparkling, like candy.

He pushed the side of my face into the glass and told me he hoped someone would see us. We were far enough up I thought it unlikely, so let him. I am making it sound like I didn't like it, but I liked it. He took a photo of me, before or after, I don't remember—neck and shoulders only, looking down and out at it, the Ferris wheel and the gridlock. The pastel twilight and skyline.

In the picture, I look young, hopeful, and resigned in equal measure. Lips parted, face clear, hard-won collarbone announcing itself. The face of wanting without knowing what to want.

It was fall, we were Floridians, and Atlanta is far enough north for the foliage to be different, for the trees to wear colors we couldn't see at home. So we went to the botanical garden and walked through the oak canopy, suspended on a hanging path.

We wound down into the center of the trees, back to Earth. Fall is a descriptor: the leaves fell and we spun around in them, together and alone. He was smiling at me, I remember. I took out my phone to get a video, the brown-red fluttering and flooding around us. Blood on the trees, blood on the ground; the blood in our bodies, still.

He's not in the video. I'm not, either. I can't find it, but I remember how it went: he says *I love you, Jamie* and I say it back, but there's a pause.


Have I told you about the time I arrived in Lisbon, alone and sleepless? About how I sobbed in the hostel living room, waiting to go to bed? I hadn't slept for 36 hours; padded off the plane hungover on bad trans-Atlantic redeye wine I'd drunk—as usual, then—without dinner. It was the first time I'd ever traveled alone.

When I landed: the sudden and acute foreignness of it all. The way an unknown language commands the ears, forces you to listen. It was in the smallest things: the electrical outlets, the toilets, all different but only just. Like walking out onto a different planet—or a dream version of this one.

Or maybe I was just 24 and scared.

I sat there for an hour that felt like four. Across the ocean, everyone who loved me was asleep. As the Portuguese day ticked closer to noon, I called my parents; called the man I was already thinking of as my ex. They all told me to get some sleep, that once I woke up, I'd be fine.

They were right. And the experience intoxicated me, taught me almost too well how to be alone. But my fear, in that first moment; the feeling of utter unbelonging and singularity. I thought the ground would open up and swallow me. Wanted it to.

What am I doing, writing you this story? What am I trying to say to you?

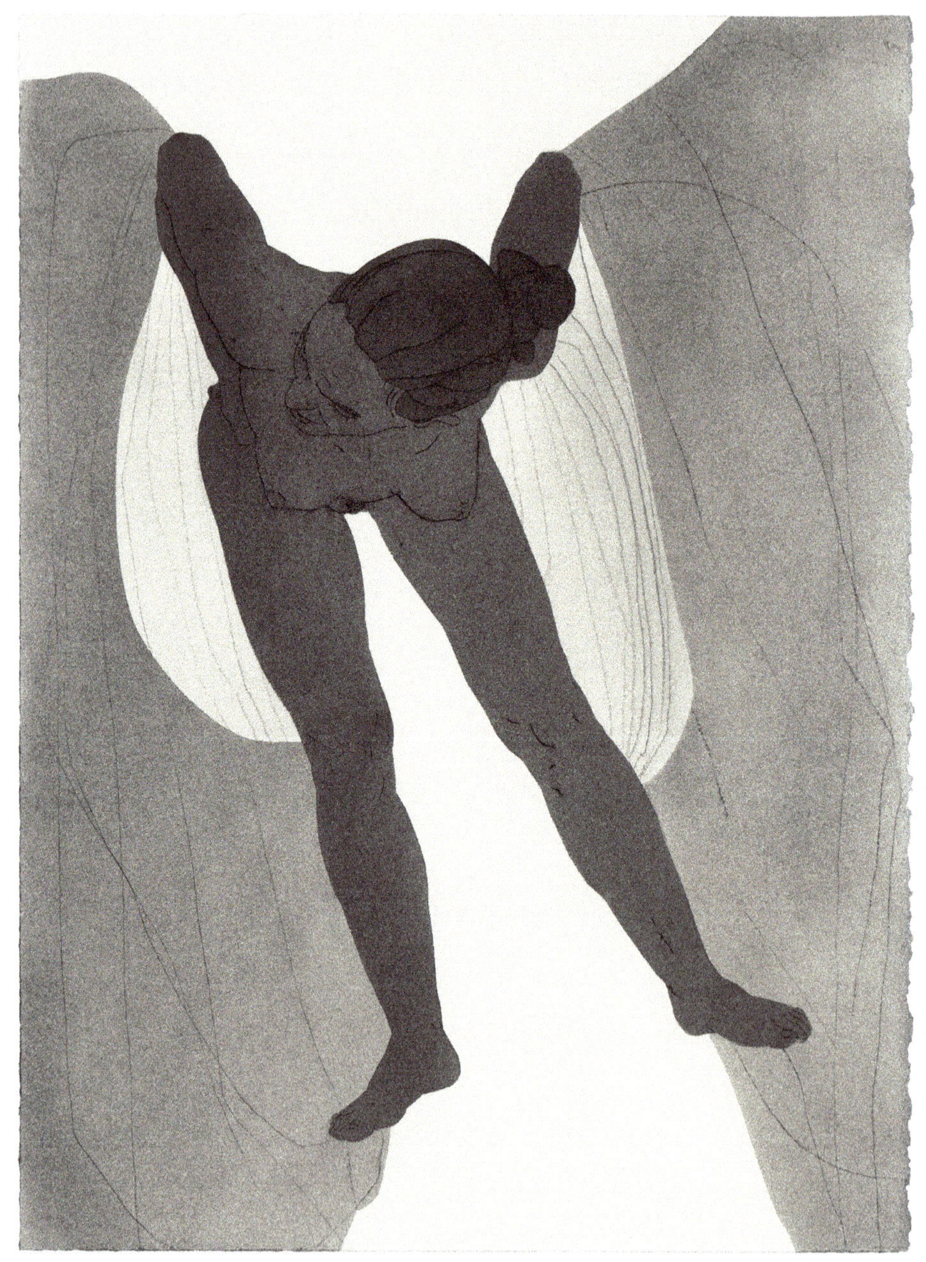



*Crossing 3*

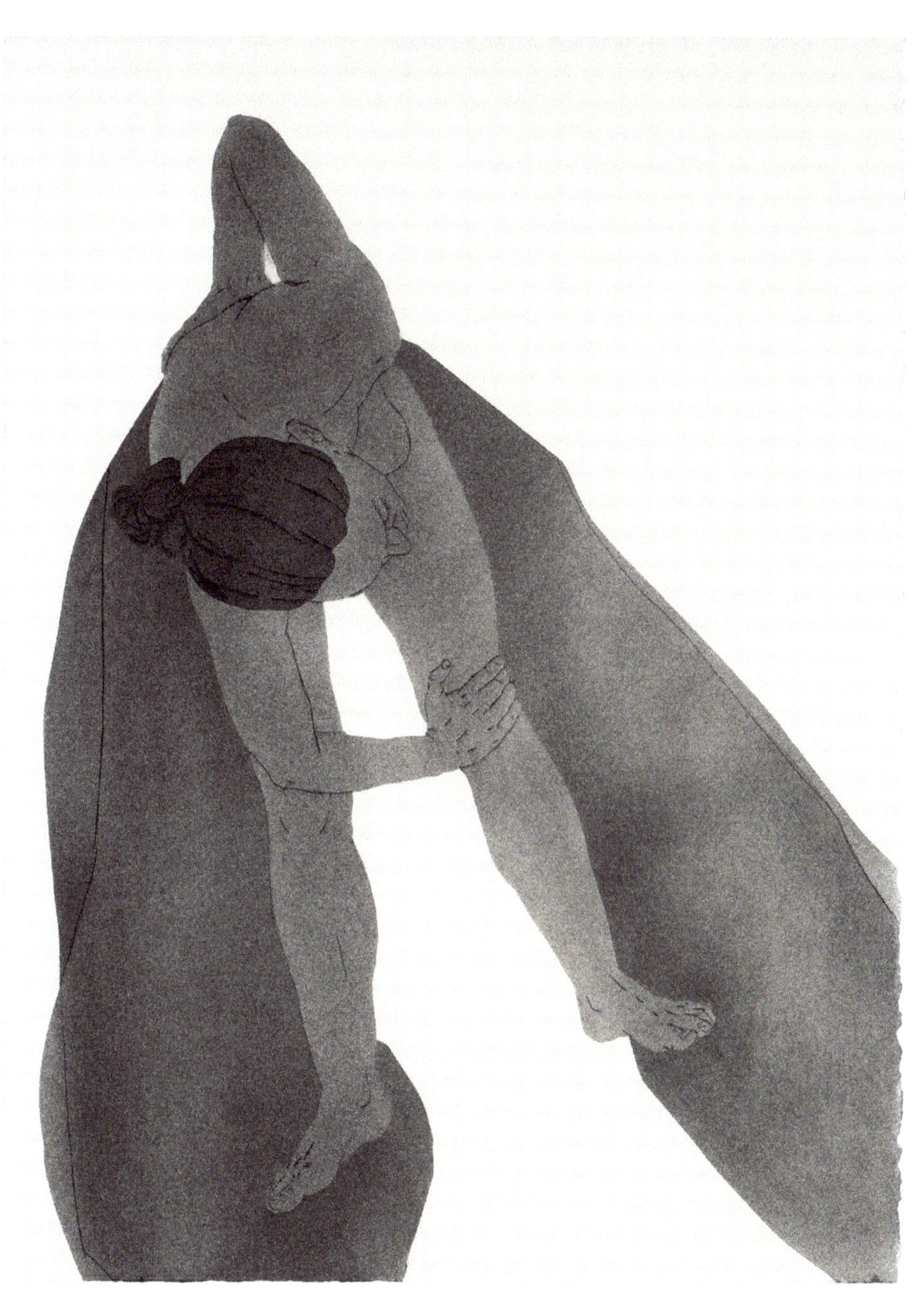

*Crossing 2*

45

Our love really was like falling: up and then down, the fall itself collapsed into heat. No time to think, or ability; nothing for anything except lying in the sun-flooded bed with you, dappled—your arms, your breasts. Your skin.

Then every next thing we did was the best one: the song we wrote based on your daughter's drawing, a rough toddler scrawl she'd titled *Sad Person*. Planning an absurd picnic as we zipped down a northern Arizona highway after dark, trying to keep ourselves awake. Memorizing each other's east-coast phone numbers on the edge of the Grand Canyon, then slow dancing there under moon-shot starlight. Wandering through Walmart to shop for the end of the world together.

The immediacy of it, the instant sense of home—though there was always some sort of chaos. Your house felt like catastrophe christmas: love's soft frustrations; toys all over the floor. The smell of us, glistening, smeared on each other's faces. A thing that couldn't have been hoped for.

The vanishing half-life of it, the cracked-egg fragility. The way it began to cleave itself apart as soon as it was. Like the question of time itself and what it means, its nature.

Like the look of mistrust over your shoulder as you walked up the stairs, silent. It had been two months. Eight weeks. Barely enough time to mend a bone.

These, our bodies, powered by our delicate blood. Bodies come and go, like all of it.

The end of the world was like the rest of it: not, until it was. And then it was, and then we were holed up in your house with its pink toys and shag carpet, with the cat hair passing through like tumbleweeds. I listened to your coffeemaker belch in the mornings and sneaked downstairs to stare at the dying world outside the window.

Your window, suddenly, ours. Far too soon, though I'd comforted myself by saying it was temporary: a pandemic-sponsored version of a lesbian stereotype. We thought, like everyone else, it would take two weeks, maybe three.

Our bed, a bed you bought when you hoped not to touch your then-wife in the night by accident. I blinked awake, apart from you; thought, *my woman bought a king-sized bed to sleep comma-curled on its edge*. Then I covered the distance, tucked my hands under the fold of your breasts, and pulled the small swell of your belly to me.

You could call it a culling, the way a love song gets so quickly swallowed. The way I stood on rocks and roads, from coast to coast, alone. Driving myself east along the gorge—away. Then back again.

It's an apocalypse narrative whether you like it or not: the earthworms on the asphalt innumerable, as if they'd been rained there. The flags peeking from trailer windows, motley. All of us locked in.

This isn't about death. At least, not more so than anything else.

I don't know exactly when it changed, how it happened so quickly. The way you spit at me like a stranger.

I sat there staring at the stranger of you, wondering if you remembered when you said it: *it's like I can't get close enough.* How we could barely keep our hands off each other long enough to finish a meal.

It didn't last long. And I'd always had doubts: the small way you looked at me, the space you'd keep between our knees when you sat beside me. And then the hours I spent wanting the day gone, waiting for our romance to restart.

The slow-paced darkness, and you still sitting across from me, as far away on the couch as you could. You didn't think about it, you said—nothing drove you to the nectar of it anymore: your hands in my hair. Your lips on my lips. Our skins endless. Your body like mine, but not; so much easier for me to call *perfect.* The way you'd looked at the new expanse of my body and, in pleasure, groaned.

Before I met you, I'd worked to keep my life free of complications: no kids, no pets, no serious connections. Nothing of sustenance or substance. Nothing to make me grow roots.

I was living clean, I thought. And narrow. I coiled in so tightly on myself that my very blood stopped.

So to realize the truth of it: all reward in mess, all experience in flesh, the cacophony of abundance. That our bodies do stop, even if we offer them fulfillment. That we can only ever be so much.

So I made brownies with your daughter—picked her up so she could pour the flour in. We licked the batter off the whisk together. Later, I turned my face toward the noise of her crying. I got out of bed to feed your yowling cat.

Then, for one sweet hour, I folded myself around your body, the blankets covered in dog hair. The warmth of you in sleep: how it grew. Like the opposite of entropy.

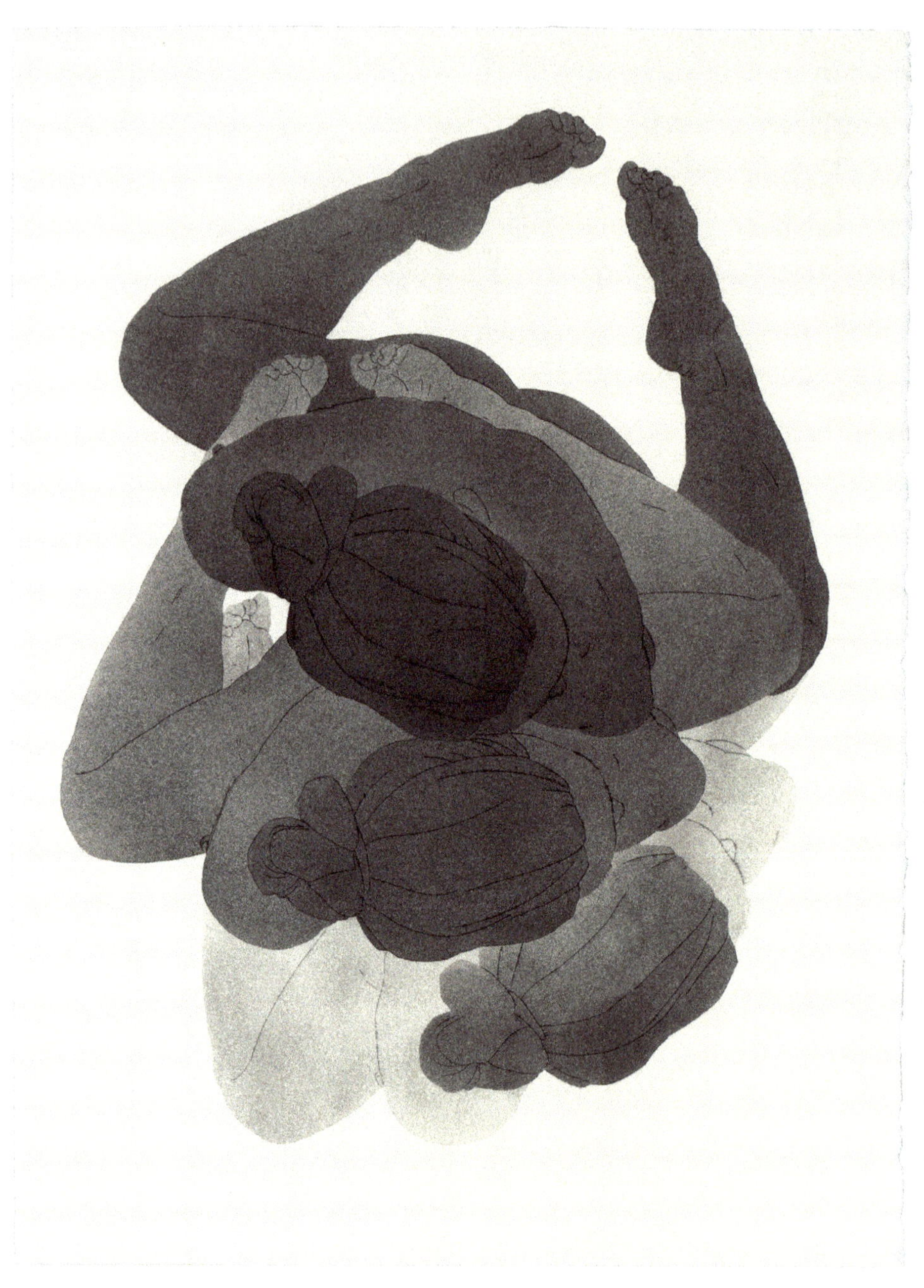



Crossing 4

We pulled on each other's faces, grimaced. We whispered to each other: *prove yourself.*

There were days I didn't want to talk to you. Didn't want to talk about it. There were days I was disturbed by my own face; still am.

The sag of the skin, inevitable. The span, untenable. My perfectionism thwarted by the fact of flesh.


How I pulled myself down the stairs, slow—not looking at you, but thinking. The things I'd imagine asking for.

I ran them through my head, the options: you pulling my hair not with passion, but intention; slapping me across the face. You calling me *ugly little bitch* while you fucked me.

You wouldn't; you'd never. You'd tell me and I'd know it to be true. But that didn't make me want it any less—that thing that isn't talking but doing. That thing that I thought would say everything that needs to be said.

We walked through that house, made love, or made laughter. The dishes, the dog. The dust.

We pulled on each other's faces, grimaced. We whispered to each other: *prove yourself.*


Here in this place she calls the wrong side of the Mississippi, I catalog the things I miss about my mother: afternoon coffee and crossword puzzles; plastic-bag-mise-en-place, all the vegetables chopped and stored as soon as they're bought. She stands there over the cutting board and calls it therapy, the wet line of the knife on the wood.

One day, I rode my bike to the end of the asphalt and sat down where the trail met the road. *What do I do, mama? What do I do?*

*What can you do?* she said. *Try not to get hit by a bus.*


I sail east toward the mountain, remembering it's there and—for now, for a while—will be. I climb her halfway, come to the shadow, the side where water always runs.

A slug hauls itself across the footpath, vulnerable and unctuous. I look at the river, turn around.


I was so bad at staying in one place until I wasn't. I was bad even at homeostasis: ten states in seven days; bootprints in uphill mud after an hour on the elliptical. Running, literally, on empty.

Then I fell into the soft of it—the rivulet…………

50

Then I fell into the soft of it—the rivulet and gunnel of you, the thick. I dove. I breathed into your face in a world with fraught breathing: with every breath, you might catch. You might transmit.

*When I was a baby. When I was your age. When I was someone I understood.*

The hours dripped by slowly, but somehow stacked up all at once—not enough of them by far. The television, the shower curtain, the stains on the couch. Sometimes I think about it, the gestalt of us, our neon trajectories racing around that house in fast forward: crying and then laughing on the floor of your office, crushed together pouring out *I love yous* in bed. Screaming at each other in the stairwell. Trying.

If someone could tell you your future, would you listen? Could you? Could you bear to know the end before living the story itself? To know the ugly truth of it, how closeness can collapse into distance, like a canyon carved? How sometimes, it's built to?

I wonder if I will tell you again, someday, how I loved the flickering light of you—the woman who taught me to love women. Who shattered me whole.

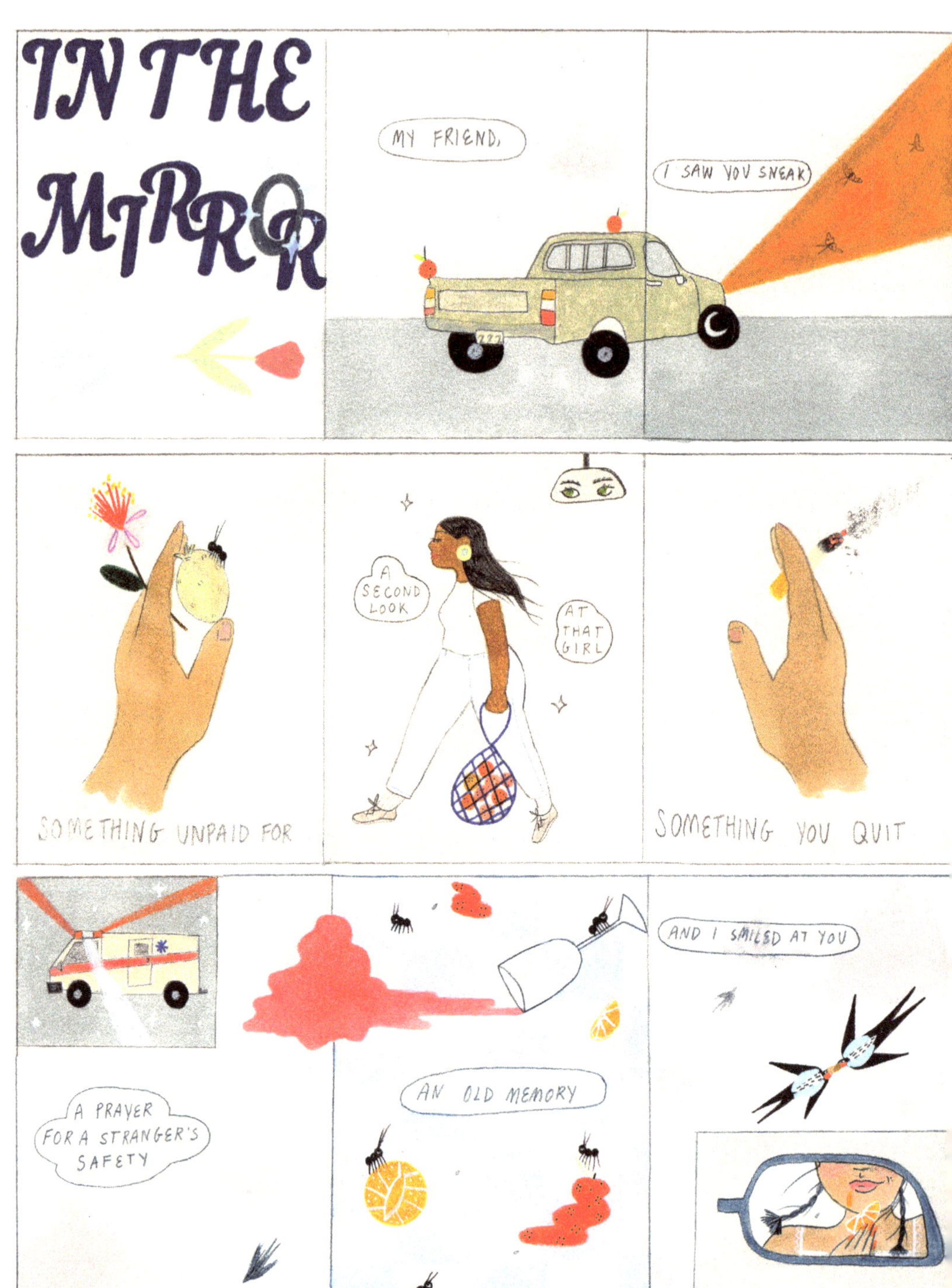

IN THE MIRROR
MY FRIEND,
I SAW YOU SNEAK
SOMETHING UNPAID FOR
A SECOND LOOK
AT THAT GIRL
SOMETHING YOU QUIT
A PRAYER FOR A STRANGER'S SAFETY
AN OLD MEMORY
AND I SMILED AT YOU

# IN THE MIRROR

Comic by Ree Artemisa

# MIND

# THE

Creative Non-Fiction by Anita Macauley

# ING

# G A P:

## the Future of the Burnside Bridge

Photography by Goldandfaceted

In late summer 1999, we moved into an apartment complex wedged between the Willamette River and Union Station in downtown Portland. It was a gritty bit of land on the west bank of the river, with a tiny dock near a stretch of polluted sand just north of the Steel Bridge. It was a weird time to be living in downtown Portland, and it was a weird address. It was not an upscale neighborhood. In fact, it wasn't really a neighborhood at all, just a strip of apartments along the riverbank. Technically a part of the River District, it was cut off from the other residential areas by railroad tracks. Our neighbors were bank tellers and receptionists and new graduates like us. The building, constructed in the early 1980s, had pressed wood kitchen cabinets and beige carpet. Its one luxury was a pocket door that could be pulled closed over our bedroom window to dull the sound of the Amtrak and Union Pacific trains rolling past.

We moved there because we felt it brought us closer to the things we found interesting about Portland at that time—shows at Berbati's Pan, drinks at Shanghai Tunnel, morning runs in Waterfront Park, Saturday Market. We didn't realize we were moving into a construction zone, or that over the next few years our choice of neighborhood would give us a front row seat to the construction of the northern end of the city.

One winter evening, while on a dog walk, we happened upon the recently dismantled Lovejoy Columns stacked in the rail yard adjacent to Naito Parkway. Anyone who has lived in Portland for a while knows the Lovejoy Columns have attained near urban legend status. In the late 1940s bored train watchman Tom Stefopoulos decided to use the pausing trains as a perch from which to paint bright images; chalk-white owls, trees, and Greek philosophers. The soot-blackened underside of the Lovejoy Viaduct made a perfect canvas for his copperplate, calligrapher style. The resulting effect was a sort of DIY cathedral populated by mythical characters. The underside of the Lovejoy Viaduct has been memorialized in pop culture history. You can still catch a glimpse of how the columns looked in an Elliott Smith video ("Lucky Three"), or the beginning of the movie *Drugstore Cowboy*. Although there were many efforts to preserve the columns, only remnants were saved; you can view them at Elizabeth Plaza on NW 10th Avenue in the Pearl District. As poetic as the columns were, Lovejoy Viaduct was problematic for developers because it was standing in the way of buildable land just north of the city center—the area we now know as the northernmost end of the Pearl District.

During those months after the Viaduct came down, we would take long walks through this construction zone, as condos sprung up seemingly overnight. What used to be empty rail yard was now covered with new sidewalks and green parking meters. We were captivated by the new Portland that was materializing around us. We read in the papers that the developers had modeled the Pearl's condos after the five-story Haussmannian style buildings in Paris; a city that was rebuilt on top of its razed medieval predecessor. After work we would go for walks to look at these new buildings, watching as blocks and courtyards formed and streetlights were installed and turned on. Watching the flurry of it all being built so quickly made an impression; it threw everything about Portland as we knew it into stark relief. The places we frequented suddenly appeared gritty and (literally) covered in a patina; regular everyday Portland shopfronts with wood-paned windows now quaint. Everything seemed to grow a layer of moss overnight. And with this new perspective we seemed to be able to appreciate the historic Portland even better. We marveled as each new building went up; awed not by the architecture—but because we felt we were witnessing something from its beginning.

### The Steel Bridge

One of my favorite moments in the Steel Bridge's cultural history was the time Phoenix (an indie synth-rock band from Versailles, France) chose the Steel Bridge bike path as a location for a promotional video, the four band members cycling across during cherry blossom season on a beautiful sunny day in March 2013. In the video, the band pedals under the delicate pink blossoms of the adjacent Waterfront Park and the camera follows as they enter the bike path on the lower deck of the Steel Bridge.

Watching this scene gave me a new appreciation for the bridge; I could see it through a visitor's eyes for what it was—an urban planning triumph—a draw for visitors and a river crossing connected so seamlessly to the adjacent Waterfront Park it requires barely any pedaling. It is arguably one of the best biking experiences to be had in our city. When you bike across the Steel on the lower deck, there is a feeling of gliding barely above water. Arriving on the eastside, you shoot out onto the Eastbank promenade into a panorama of downtown Portland cityscape and watery reflections, as if you've entered an urban watercolor painting. As you pedal south on the Eastbank, downtown comes into full view, tucked behind the pink-blossomed cloak of the Waterfront Park. The bike path was added to the lower deck of the Steel Bridge in 2001. But during the time we lived next to the Steel, there was no pedestrian bridge on the lower deck for foot traffic or bikes. There were only lonely freight trains and the occasional Amtrak. Living next to the Steel Bridge was to appreciate the hub of activity it represented and to consider its working quality. It was designed to allow cargo ships to pass under its

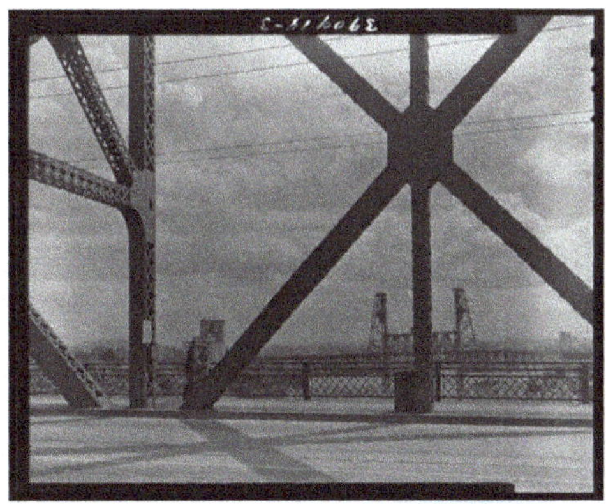

*The Steel Bridge from the Broadway, Sept. 1939* (Org Lot 52 No. 390918-3)

*Sternwheeler passing through the Steel Bridge, Sept. 1939* (Org Lot 52 No. 390913-3)

*Courtesy of OHS Digital Collections*

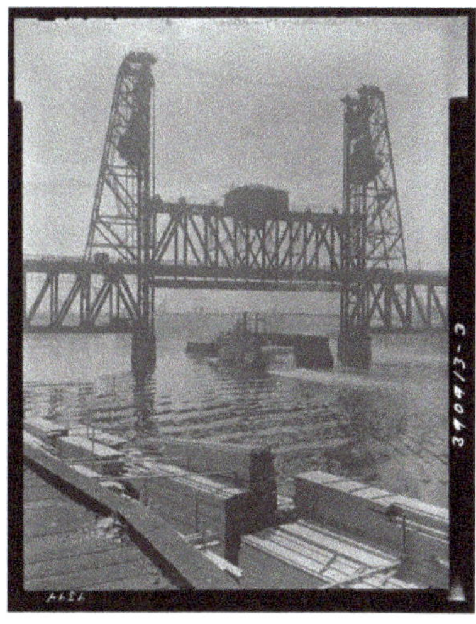

57

central span; to carry train, car, streetcar, bike, and foot traffic. *The Oregonian* has called it "the hardest working bridge of the Willamette."

If you have never spent time in proximity to bridges, or you're just in the habit of using them to get somewhere else, it can be shocking to see steel and concrete suddenly churn into motion. During the three years we lived in that riverside apartment, we had a front-seat view to the workings of the Steel Bridge. We watched as river traffic moved up and down the Willamette, triggering bridge openings for the larger vessels. A loud bell would clang several times to alert foot and auto traffic of an impending lift. Then a continuous high-pitched bell sounded as the street was closed. We could watch from our deck as the center span rose while the two 800-to-900-ton counterweights, connected via cables, slowly lowered to just above street level. It was like living next to a giant steel creature with an impeccably hinged mechanical jaw. Fully raised, it allows enough clearance for cargo ships to pass—165 feet in total. It loomed over our apartment, blackening the sky when raised and creating a squared aperture through which you could imagine what a bridgeless Willamette River might have looked like. Then, with a dull rumble, the deck of the upper bridge would lumber back into place.

There were the days where the bridge played tricks on us; we would wake to see the bottom of the Steel Bridge completely obscured by fog; then, minutes later, like a magic trick, the sun would burn through and the bridge would slowly come back into the visible world.

**Ghost Bridges of the Willamette** · · · · · · · · · · · · · · · · · · · · · · · · · · · · · · · · · ·
When you're young, you tend to think of the built environment as immutable. Bridges stay put. In most people's collective memory (those born after the mid 1970s, at least) the bridges we know today have always existed. The Fremont Bridge, built in 1973, is the youngest of the seven bridges visible from the city center that cross the Willamette. The Sellwood Bridge was replaced in 2015, but of the bridges visible from the city center that cross the Willamette, there have been no major demolitions since the 1905 Morrison was replaced in 1958.

A longer view of history reveals bridges that existed before the nine bridges that now cross the Willamette River near the city center; they were made of less durable materials and degraded or were consumed by fires. There are historic photos of the Willamette River that are like puzzles—multiple spans of historic bridges that no longer exist can be seen layered on top of each other. The first incarnation of the Steel Bridge, constructed in 1888 in nearly the same location as the current bridge, was built to accommodate foot and horse-drawn streetcars on top, and train traffic below. The Morrison Bridge, the first bridge across the Willamette, started out as a wood swing span structure in 1887 and was replaced twice—once in 1905 and once in 1958. You can find photos online of the 1905 Morrison next to the 1958 Morrison before the older bridge was eventually demolished.

When you consider that the first five bridges built in Portland, between the years 1887 (Morrison, of iron and wood) and 1894 (the original Burnside, built from wrought iron and steel) are no longer in existence, you can appreciate that while we live in a city where much of the built structures of Victoriana still endure, there are a lot of ghosts here too. Among these ghost bridges were the swing bridges, built with a center span that swung out like a fence door, to accommodate large ships. If you want to see a cool

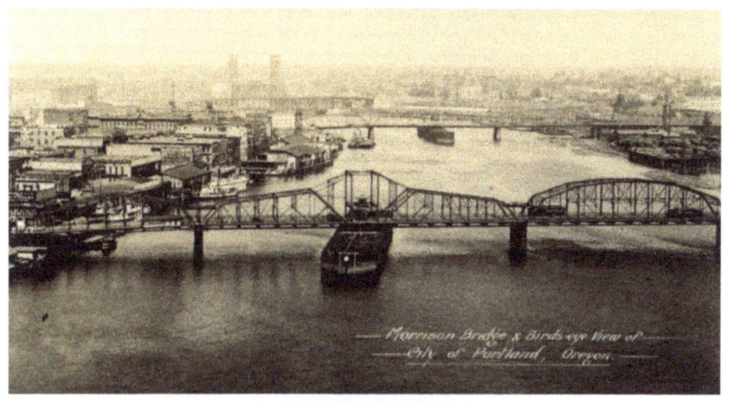

*Old Morrison Bridge with ship* (A2004-002.577)
*Steel Bridge, circa Dec. 1890* (A2004-002.3630)
*Courtesy of Portland Archives and Records Center*

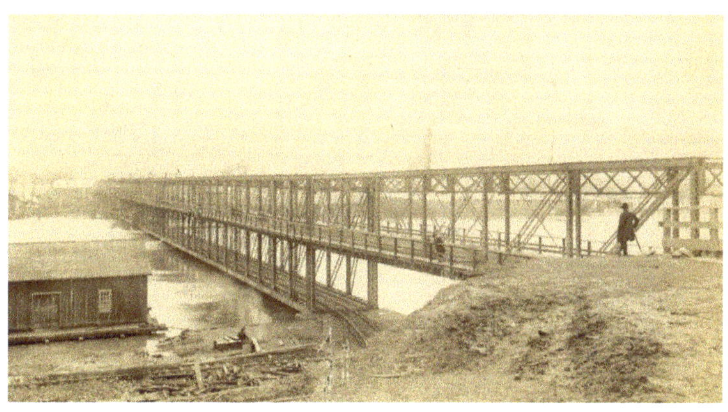

depiction of these swing span bridges, you can go to a bar called Solo Club in Slabtown with a wall mural titled "Portland, Oregon and Surroundings, 1890" that depicts the Steel, Burnside, and Morrison bridges in their swing span eras; in 1890, the Hawthorne Bridge hadn't been built yet. Swing span designs were constructed on a central pier, which essentially halved the size of the river. For these reasons, the swing span design gave way to the more modern lift and bascule types we see today.

In the comments section on the Vintage Portland website, people say that you can use Google Maps to see the historic pier footings of the original 1888 Steel Bridge, which still exist, underwater. It's interesting to think of bridges—seemingly durable parts of our everyday lives, as ephemera.

## The Burnside

In Spring of 2024, Burnside Bridge is a bit of a forgotten place, cycling-wise. The bike lane is separated from the traffic lanes by a rickety row of plastic delineators; and once you're in the lane, you can't easily stop to check out the sights; you'd need to pick up your bike and step up onto the sidewalk. The bike lanes are still covered in gravel from the past winter's storms; the freeway is loud, and even without the recent street

# It's interesting to think of parts of our everyday

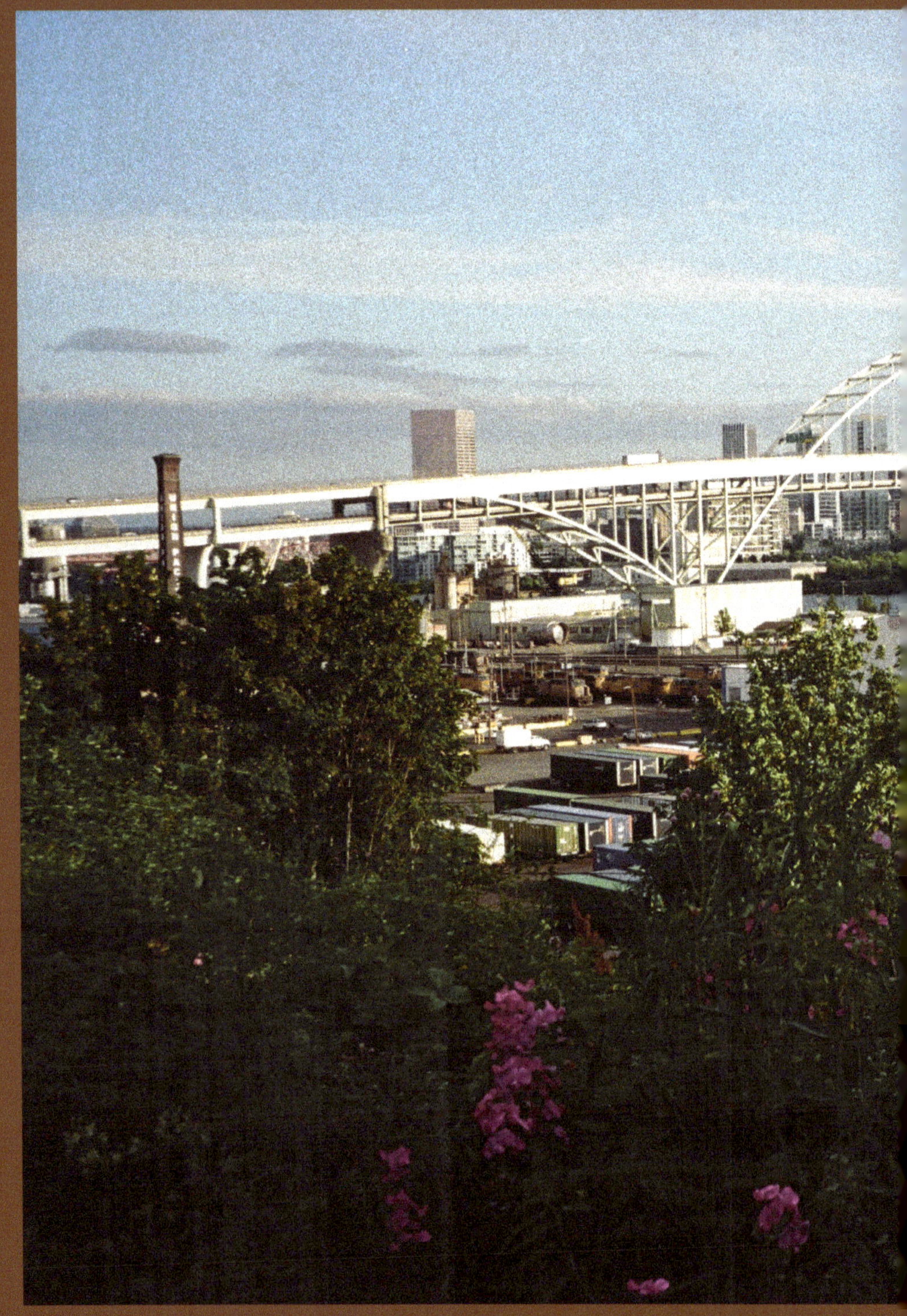

bridges—seemingly durable
lives, as ephemera.

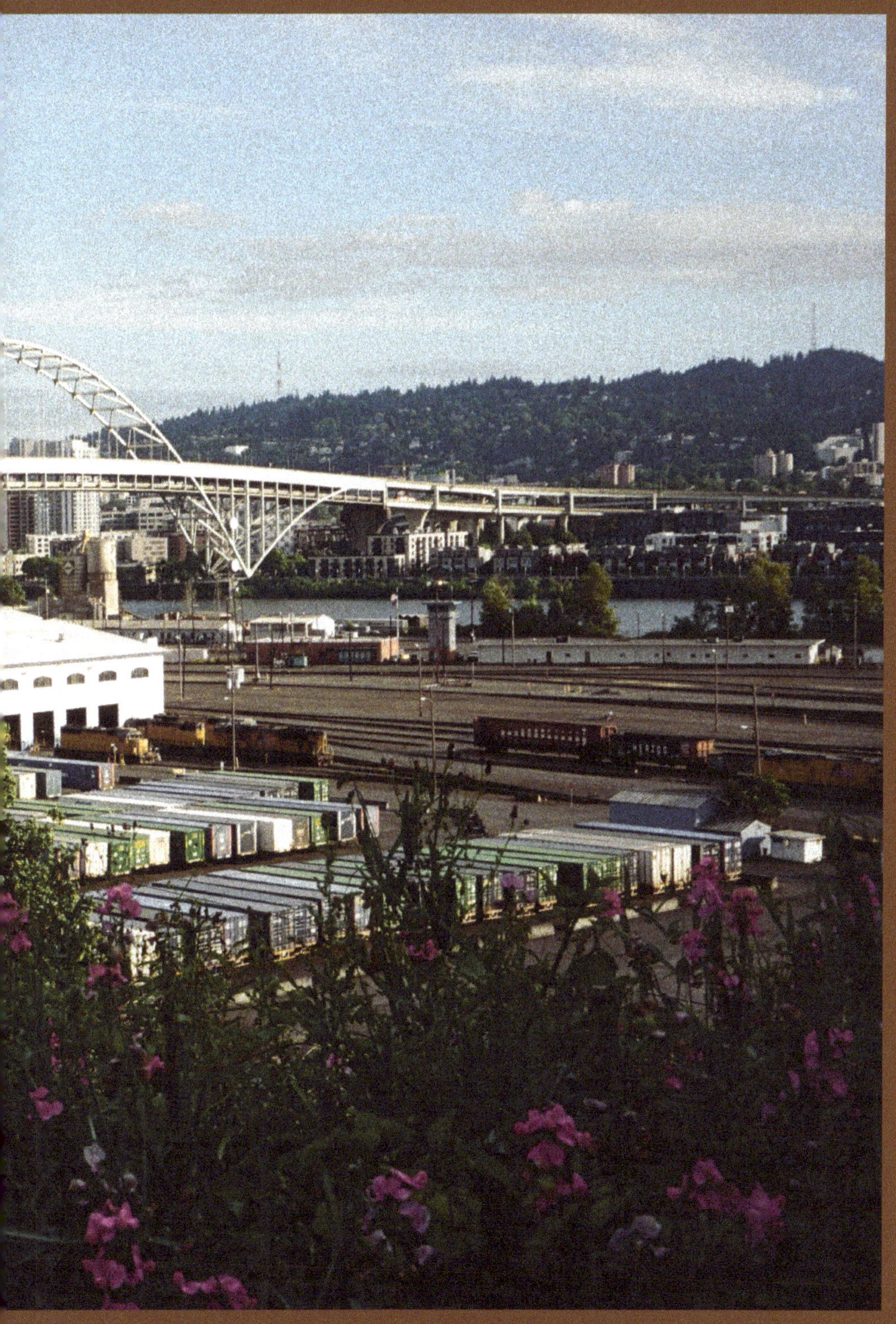

race takeovers, it's one of the more precarious bridges to cycle over. The bridge's only connectivity to the Eastbank Esplanade is via a scary four-flight staircase that is rarely used. The metal staircase on the west side leading down to NW First Avenue is not ideally located either. Even in daylight hours, the staircase is heavily shaded by the buildings and the bridge itself. Although a useful shortcut to quickly access Old Town-Chinatown, carrying a bike up or down these stairs is difficult.

The derelict feeling of crossing the Burnside by bike is also reflected in the statistics for cycling from the previous year. Portland Bureau of Transportation's recently released 2023 Portland Bicycle Counts report shows bike counts "slightly increased from 2022 levels but still down substantially compared to pre-pandemic years." But the Burnside Bridge, despite its problems, is still a place that draws people. On an April evening this year, I biked down to the bridge to see if I could catch the sunset. I noticed a group of kids on scooters, pausing to have their photos taken. It is the crossing that divides the city into four quadrants, and it serves as one of the most iconic vantage points to view the neon *Portland, Oregon* sign presiding from atop the historic White Stag block in Old Town. The centrality of the 1,382-foot-long structure is such that every plane of it is culturally significant; The underside of the Burnside Bridge has served as the home of the Saturday Market since the 1970s, and on the West side, historic districts hug either side of the bridge (Old Town-Chinatown and the Japanese American Historical Plaza).

The bridge has played a central role in the history of our city. According to a presentation put together by a team examining the aesthetic qualities of the Burnside, the 1926 bridge we know today was originally envisioned for streetcars, and in its nearly 100 years of existence, has witnessed numerous significant cultural events starting with union strikes in the 1930s and most recently, the "die-in" of 2020 to protest George Floyd's murder.

Both ends of the Burnside Bridge have played an important role in forming Portland's 1990s DIY culture. At its east end, a mural on the building that housed the former Disjecta arts center, reads "Long Live the Wildcards, Misfits, & Dabblers" in stark black and white block font. Underneath the east end of the Burnside is the Burnside Skatepark, funded and built by skaters in 1990. At the west end of the Burnside, is the historic location of X-Ray Café, an all-ages club that existed from 1990-1994. As one of the narrators in a video created about the Café notes, "The X-Ray was physically as close to the geographical apex of the city as you could get, i.e., it was the

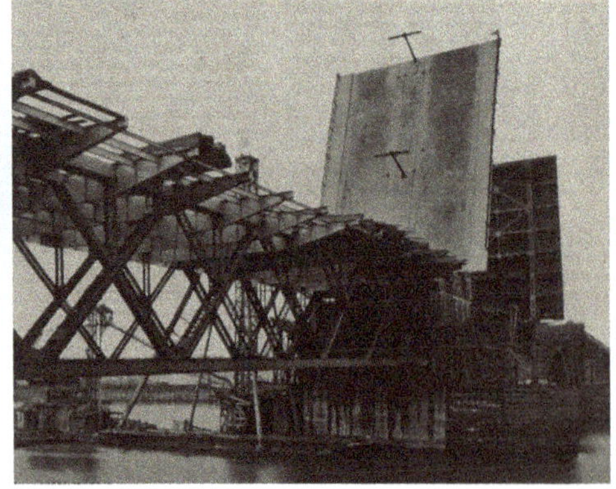

*Burnside Bridge: construction, circa Jan. 1926* (A1999-004.1149)

*Courtesy of Portland Archives and Records Center*

closest building to the middle of the Burnside Bridge, which is where east meets west and south meets north in the river." The X-Ray Café was important because it not only provided an easily accessible gathering spot for young people to experience DIY music and homegrown art; it also was enough of a presence that it actually displaced crime plaguing that part of downtown. In the documentary on the club, one of the owners notes how the club kids would go out into the street with a clown wig and a megaphone and bark at loiterers to move to the other side of the street.

I've always thought the Burnside's design elements were kind of a random pastiche. Bridges, designed by engineers, can be functionally beautiful, their every element a useful part of the design and also beautiful in their own right. The Burnside always seemed like the antithesis of this; it is squat and has the feeling of a freeway with fancy railings. In 1926, when the Burnside was completed, the City Beautiful movement was in full swing. This urban planning trend's hallmark was to borrow design details from European-style buildings, which may explain the Burnside's two different kinds of railings (cement on the outer spans and wrought iron in the middle) and its Italian-style towers. Looking more closely at the ornamental wrought iron railings, I notice that the pattern is of a square with an X in the center. Standing in the middle of the Burnside Bridge, you can't help but feel as though you are at the center of something; a middle coordinate. It makes me think of the medieval churches I studied in college art history, designed on a spiritual axis, with the nave facing east and doors facing west. These kinds of details make me second guess my assessment of the Burnside's design a little. I wonder how far we've come since City Beautiful, and whether, in contemplating a new design for the Burnside, we can honor what has been while transcending it.

## Other Crossings

On the cover of the album by the 1980s Scottish new wave band Altered Images (known best for the poppy hit "Happy Birthday") you see the band having a party on a small floating dock; in the background, two historic-looking bridges seem to layer one on top of the other. If you are prone to internet rabbit holes, you would learn the photo was taken between George V Bridge and the Second Caledonian Railway Bridge over the River Clyde in Glasgow. The First Caledonian Railway Bridge was originally constructed in 1879 and replaced in 1967; except that, curiously, the bridge piers of the more historic bridge were left intact, so that today, the new 1967 bridge coexists with the 1879 piers next to it. In addition to serving as a backdrop for new wave band album covers, the bridge and piers, artifacts of the 1879 structure, serve as a reminder of the historical crossing. In the 1980s, these piers were covered with Greek inscriptions and took on a new life as public art. Murals cover the street side views of the Second Caledonian Railway Bridge so that the whole area feels like a pleasing jumble—of new and old, and art on top of history.

Glasgow, Scotland, like Portland, Oregon is a city of bridges—16 bridges cover its River Clyde. One of them, the Albert Bridge, constructed in 1871, has riveted lower arches painted an olive green that recall the surrounding foliage. Its upper deck is ornamented with wrought iron streetlamps, and its piers feature medallions of the bust of Queen Victoria and Prince Albert. In 2016, the bridge was restored, and a peeling iron coat of arms bearing the inscription "Let Glasgow Flourish" was repainted in striking colors. Another well-loved Glasgowian bridge, the Tradeston Bridge (nicknamed the Squiggly Bridge) was constructed in 2009. The Squiggly Bridge, so named because it cants upward in a curved shape to give room for ships to pass underneath, is a pedestrian-only bridge and was built partly to revitalize the Tradeston district by connecting it with a financial district.

Paris is another city of bridges. There are 37 bridges crossing the Seine, with no less than six pedestrian bridges, or "passerelles." The Passerelle Simone-de-Beauvoir, constructed in 2006, is one of its most modern. Constructed by the Eiffel Company (a descendant of the same firm who built the Eiffel Tower) the bridge is a trippy lens-shaped structure with upper and lower decks, multiple perspective points from which to view Paris's landmarks, and a central space for events to be held. It connects the National Library and the Parc de Bercy district on the right bank. Another of Paris's bridges, the Pont des Arts (the famous "love locks" bridge) was originally constructed in 1804. It is one of Paris's most beautiful. Designed to resemble a hanging garden, it is a beloved crossing with trees and park benches and places to sit and eat a leisurely lunch. Artists and musicians can perform on this bridge in the summer.

It strikes me that although the surface design details of these structures are important, more interesting is the way a bridge allows you an opportunity for connection. Adam Gopnik, in his book about living in Paris, muses while crossing the Pont des Arts: "What truly makes Paris beautiful is the intermingling of the monumental and the personal, the abstract and the footsore particular; it and you. A city of vast and impersonal set piece architecture, it is also a city of small and intricate, improvised experience." I think that's what makes the Altered Images album cover so special. It personifies exactly what Gopnik describes; it's the small and human set against the large and communal. It is an image that captures a highly personal—and joyful—moment against an imperfect yet richly layered historical setting. It feels improvised, but that's what makes it a place worthy of an album cover, instead of just another anywhere.

## A Burnside Reimagined

The Burnside Bridge is now in the process of its own disappearing act. As part of the preparations for an earthquake-ready structure, the county will fully replace the Burnside beginning in 2027, with an expected completion in 2031. As problematic as the Burnside in its current form is for cyclists and pedestrians, I feel a kind of impending loss knowing that it will soon be replaced. I spent my early twenties walking home from work over this bridge. There is the 26-year-old me who found $40 on the stairs leading from the Burnside down to First Avenue. There is 49-year-old me, now carless after a traumatizing car accident in 2021, biking to Powell's from my house on the east side. The brutalism of car culture is amplified now that I ride my bike everywhere; pedaling to visit friends downtown or heading back home after an evening at a reading or a show. Burnside used to be a straight shot from my old apartment to inner east side venues like La Luna and later, Doug Fir, and it is still the quickest route to get from my house on the eastside to downtown.

In a city that consists mainly of a flat grid of neighborhoods hidden under tree canopies, cycling onto the Burnside gives a feeling that you are crossing into a clearing; a place where water and sky and mountains are visible all at once; where you can see things in the foreground and in the far distance at the same time. I can stop and look at the morning light hitting Big Pink. I can remind myself how many incarnations of the neon *Portland, Oregon* sign I've lived through (three). I can remember how Elliott Smith used to like walking across Portland's bridges after nights out with friends. I can smile at the fake little towers, imagining the kind of people who planned them. I still find the middle of the Burnside Bridge the best place in the city to pause, look at the West Hills, and all of the city's landmarks and crossings at once. And when I look north, in my mind's eye, beyond the Steel, the Broadway, and the Fremont, I can see my high school years in Tacoma, or further into my past: childhood, in Southeast Alaska. And by simply turning around, I can look south, and see the Morrison, Hawthorne, and Tilikum Crossing, and see my years spent as a college student at U of O. Something about the unique way the light hits and calls up memories; standing there, you feel connected to something; a citizen in a place. You can see things from the Burnside. And that feels significant, and something that shouldn't be lost.

The design phase of the new Burnside began in January 2024 and will run through early 2026. An FAQ published by the county states that "In summer 2024, the project team will ask the public for input on a range of bridge type/form options. In early-mid 2025, the project team will seek public input on additional bridge aesthetic features." In a KGW news article published in November 2023, one of the design phase project managers acknowledges the importance the design will have for Portlanders, saying: "This bridge is located in the geographic center of Portland. It is on display to everyone who travels to this region." The journalist goes on: "But that doesn't mean it's going to be an art project; the bridge suffered a funding setback with the failure of a Metro transportation ballot measure, and the county made some high-level design changes in 2021 to trim the cost from more than $1 billion down to its current level." Multnomah County's current estimated budget is $895 million for a four-lane bridge.

It's interesting that those reporting on the aesthetics of the new Burnside seem to already be bracing for an argument from Portlanders about what the future of the Burnside will look like. There has been a rich discussion among the cycling community of the concept of ramps leading to and from a new Burnside, in lieu of less desirable elevators or less accessible staircases. The spiral ramp leading from the Morrison Bridge is cited as a possible concept that could be replicated. What's clear is that the city's residents—its cyclists and pedestrians and anyone with an interest in how they will use the future bridge—hold a collective power to weigh in, not only on what the new bridge railings will look like, but on functional aspects of the structure itself.

I like to imagine what kind of design details Portlanders would impart upon their new Burnside Bridge if they were engaged with the design process. We have an opportunity, during the ongoing public input phase, to decide what it looks like. If you look at the current schematics of the replacement Burnside Bridge, shown online, you see austere gray concrete without ornamentation, something akin to the 1950s-era Morrison Bridge (the Portland bridge that most resembles a freeway overpass). There is much discussion about the width of the to-be-built Burnside Bridge, and how much room should be allowed for foot and bike traffic. With cycling numbers stagnant, the planning of the bridge could resort to cynicism if planners use the recent past as the prediction of future desire to bike the new Burnside. Right now, the preferred design plan shows a space about 14 feet wide on either side of the Burnside for bikes and pedestrians to share, separated by something transportation planners call a crash barrier. Grade separation is an important feature for bike commuting safety (separation from traffic is always preferable to no separation).

But the conversation feels like an afterthought more than a dedicated conversation about how encouraging more pedestrians and cyclists on the bridge can contribute to

It strikes me that although
of these structures are
the way a bridge allows you an

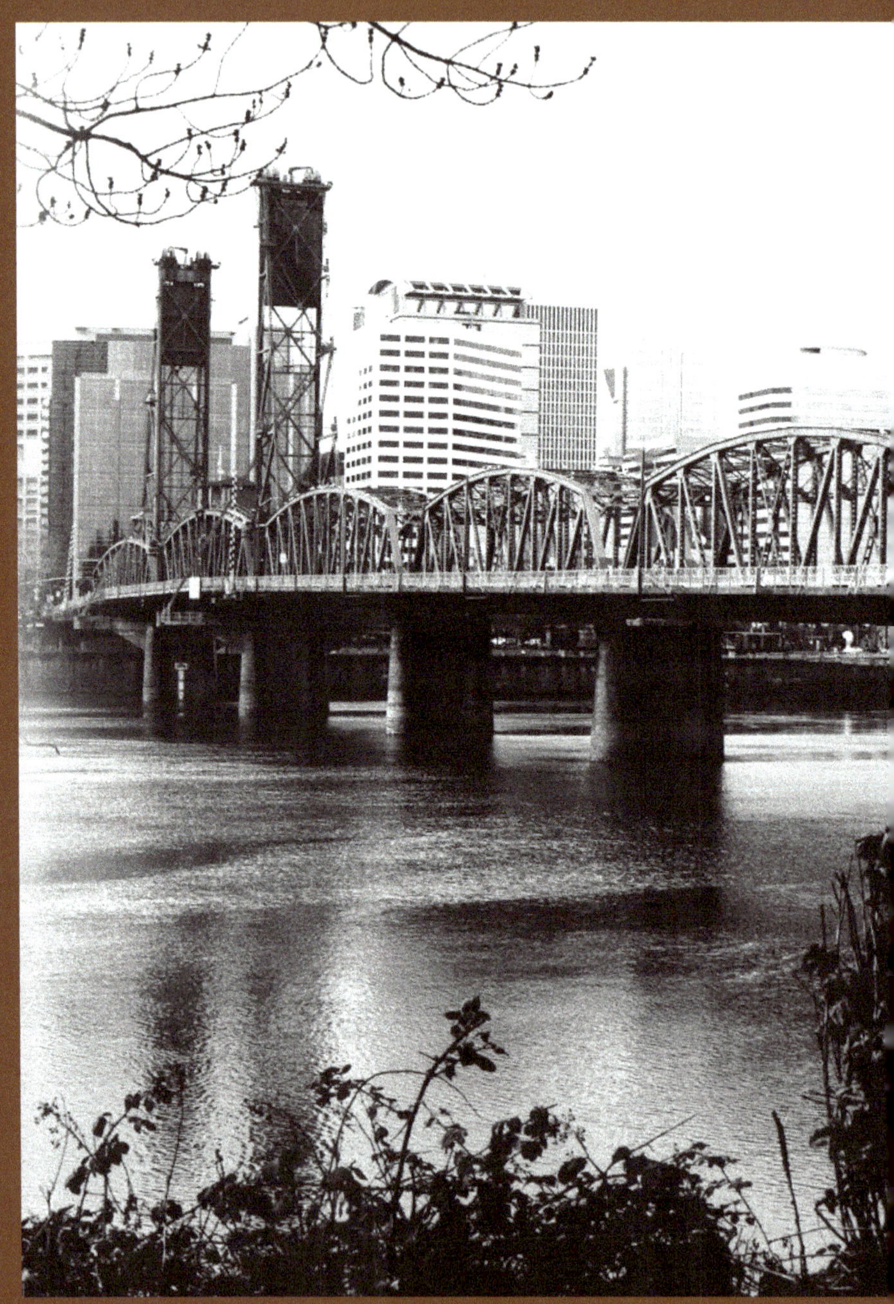

the surface design details
important, more interesting is
opportunity for connection.


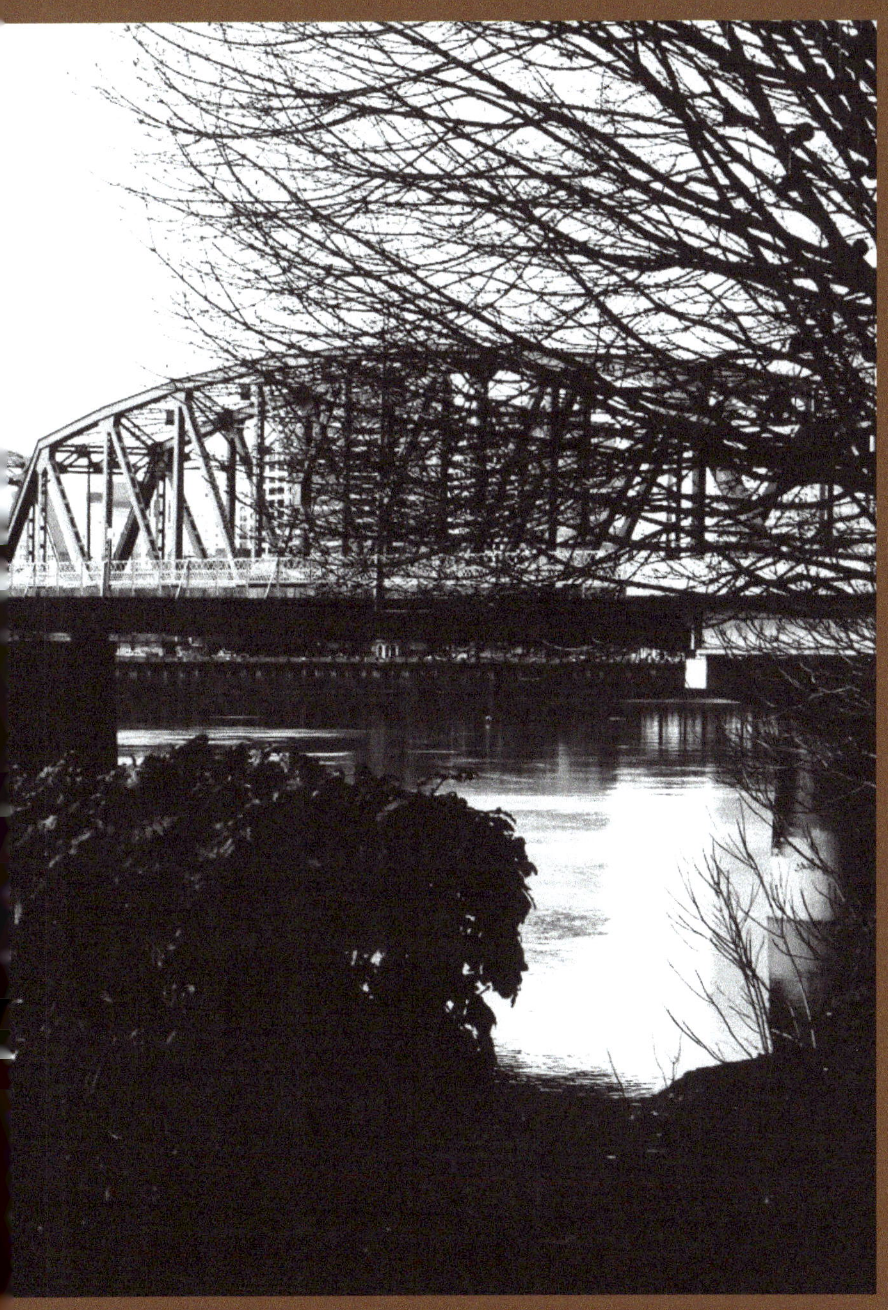

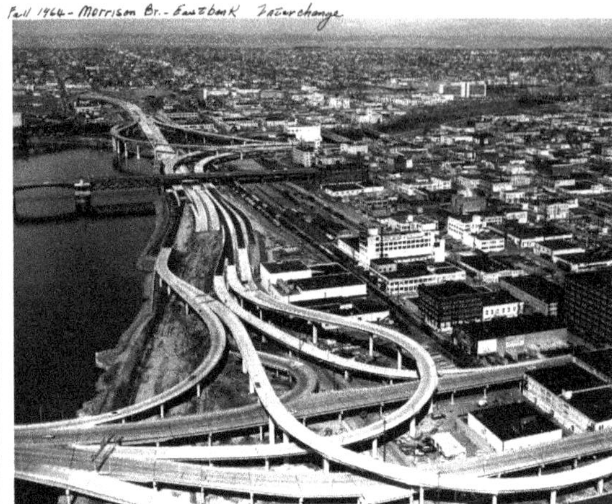


*Morrison Bridge east end Eastbank Freeway interchange, May 1964* (A2005-001.1211)

*Courtesy of Portland Archives and Records Center*

the cultural and artistic fabric of our city. There has been no discussion of the sightlines that can only be accessed while standing or cycling—not driving—on the Burnside Bridge. There has been no exploration of what it sounds like, or what it feels like, or how it could be made more enjoyable—for people, and not cars. While the public has been invited to weigh in on "design details," this loses sight of the fact that we deserve not only a safe new Burnside, but a Burnside that retains and amplifies the best of the sensory experiences we already know exist in this unique crossing at the center of our city.

What's clear is, whatever we decide collectively, the Burnside's new design will reflect what our values are. If Glasgow kept the piers of its historic railway bridge, what might we retain, if anything, of our 1926 Burnside? I think of the Burnside Skatepark, dubbed "anarchy in action" by the nonprofit that now supports it, originally funded and built by skaters without permission and endured for roughly 33 years, and wonder how the spirit of that place will be remembered. I think of the 360 Douglas Fir trees pounded into the bedrock of the river as part of the supporting pier structures, and wonder how these will figure in the story of the new Burnside and how that story will be shaped. Will we want a bridge deck we can easily walk across to get to venues that are important to us? Will the new bridge deck be appropriate to sit or lie down on, if Portlanders need to demonstrate again, as they did in 2020?

No one disputes that a new Burnside Bridge is necessary. The Burnside is a main emergency route. In 2017, *The Oregonian* shared a video created by Multnomah County that shows a simulation of what the Burnside would look like during an 8.0 magnitude earthquake: the unreinforced concrete collapsing over the west end where the MAX runs; and on the east side, the two bascule pieces of the bridge falling into the river and impeding shipping routes. The video is terrifying, and it does a good job of showing a worst-case scenario.

But the current designs we are being shown fall short, in a big way. The conversation about earthquake readiness is unquestionably important, but the designs we are being shown lack a certain kind of input, something that Portlanders know how to do intuitively: use their creative ingenuity to remake something old into something better than it was before.

What hasn't been explored or adequately discussed—yet—is the potential for the repurposing of the existing Burnside Bridge piers—either as historical artwork or as a functional part of a car-free pedestrian and bike-only crossing. If only bikes and pedestrians were to use this repurposed bridge, it could be rebuilt much lighter, and have much better connectivity to the Eastbank Esplanade.

An accessible pedestrian and bike-only path as a major component of a new Burnside Bridge, which could still carry the emergency responders and car traffic, is something we should advocate for. If you find this idea outlandish, consider how many pedestrian-only bridges have been built in the last few years to bridge the gaps in our bike and pedestrian routes. There's Tilikum Crossing (2015), the Ned Flanders Crossing over I-205 (2021), and our youngest bridge, spanning I-84, the Blumenauer Bridge (2022). We are already a city that minds its gaps; we need to apply this creativity to the design of the new Burnside that incorporates a pedestrian and bike crossing as a major component of its design and not as an afterthought.

If the Steel could have a bike path added to its lower deck years after its original construction, there is no reason the new Burnside's design shouldn't include a separate, pedestrian and bike-only space from its inception. Imagine a double-decker Burnside Bridge, where people use the lower level, like the Steel's bike path? Or a bridge where people and bikes get the top level, and cars are confined to a completely separate road underneath? Or, a Burnside with long bike and ped-only approaches, paths that diverge from the vehicle lanes, wing out over the water, via a lightweight structure that doesn't need to carry the weight of vehicles? Or, a separate floating pedestrian path, similar to the Eastbank Esplanade, that opens up like an old-style swing span? If we do not engage, we will likely get a bridge that is no more than what we require: a crossing less prone to earthquakes with cars as its main focus.

What we do not want is a bridge that doesn't serve us. City Beautiful, the planning movement that brought us the Burnside's quaint turrets, has been criticized for applying "pretty" design details somewhat haphazardly. What we don't want for the new Burnside is a structure that people don't really connect with. Absent participation in the planning process by its citizens, the new Burnside will become the Morrison Bridge's 2024 twin—a freeway-esque structure with some "prettified" details. When I think about a "new" Burnside Bridge, I can visualize its potential. But the task ahead could be fun—harnessing the collective imagination of the citizens of Portland— particularly its creative communities, who also happen to frequently be cyclists, to achieve a more functional and aesthetically pleasing Burnside.

We all stand to benefit from a pedestrian and bike-forward Burnside. Getting this from vision to reality will require funding and engineering solutions, but more than that, it requires public will. I have faith in the DIY culture of this city. We've been repurposing things for decades. There's always a gap between a vision and reality. Tom Stefopoulos, when he stepped between the rail cars to better bridge the distance from his paintbrush to the upper arches of the Lovejoy Viaduct, added to Portland's mythology with his own artistic vision, bringing it into our reality. If we step up to participate in the planning process as a city, we could collectively remake the Burnside Bridge into something we can be proud of, something that serves us all.

# VENOUS

Flash Fiction by Tracey Nguyen

# LAKE

Mixed Media by Zac Pranji

Temptation is choreographed. My sympathy is. This moment is.

What still felt real was juniper trees, sulfur water, empty road. Like I don't have to be me and the landscape could care less.

What's presented now soothes in an immediate way. Beauty of this soaking creature, music jumping out the bathtub. Dim-lit, smoky second floor.

Bodies of water, arterial. It always comes back to this, regardless of city. If industrial, a permanent ache. A semblance of recognition when really, no moment is like any other at all.

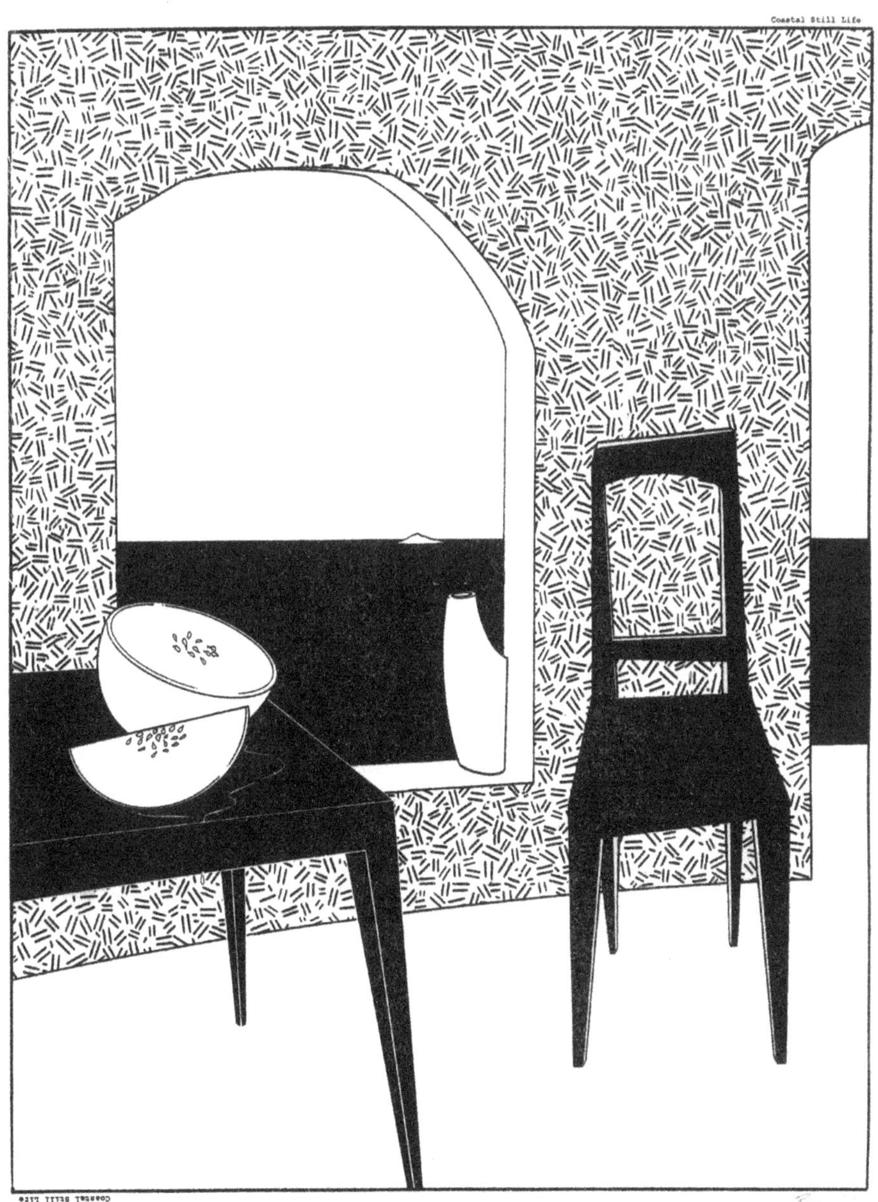

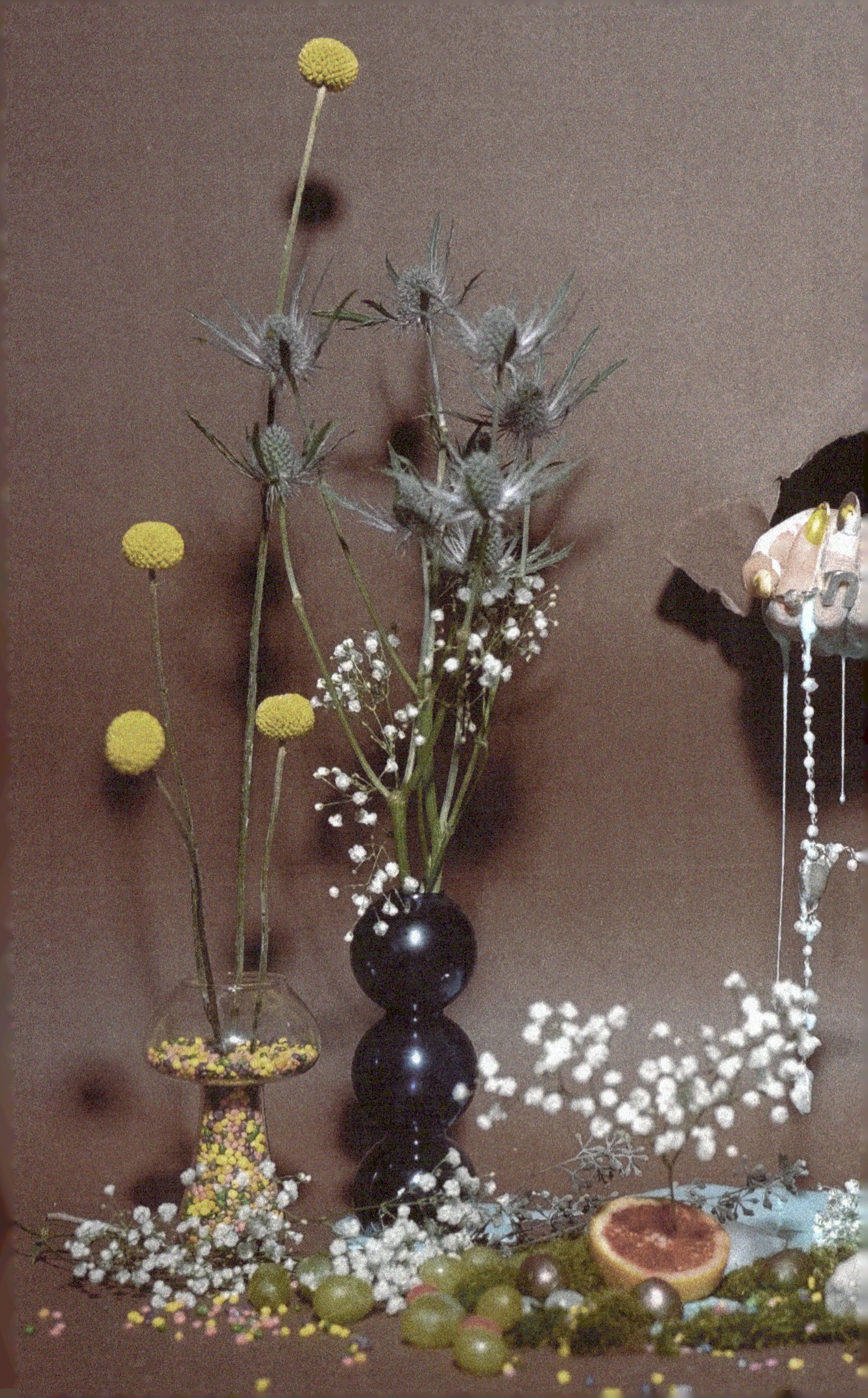

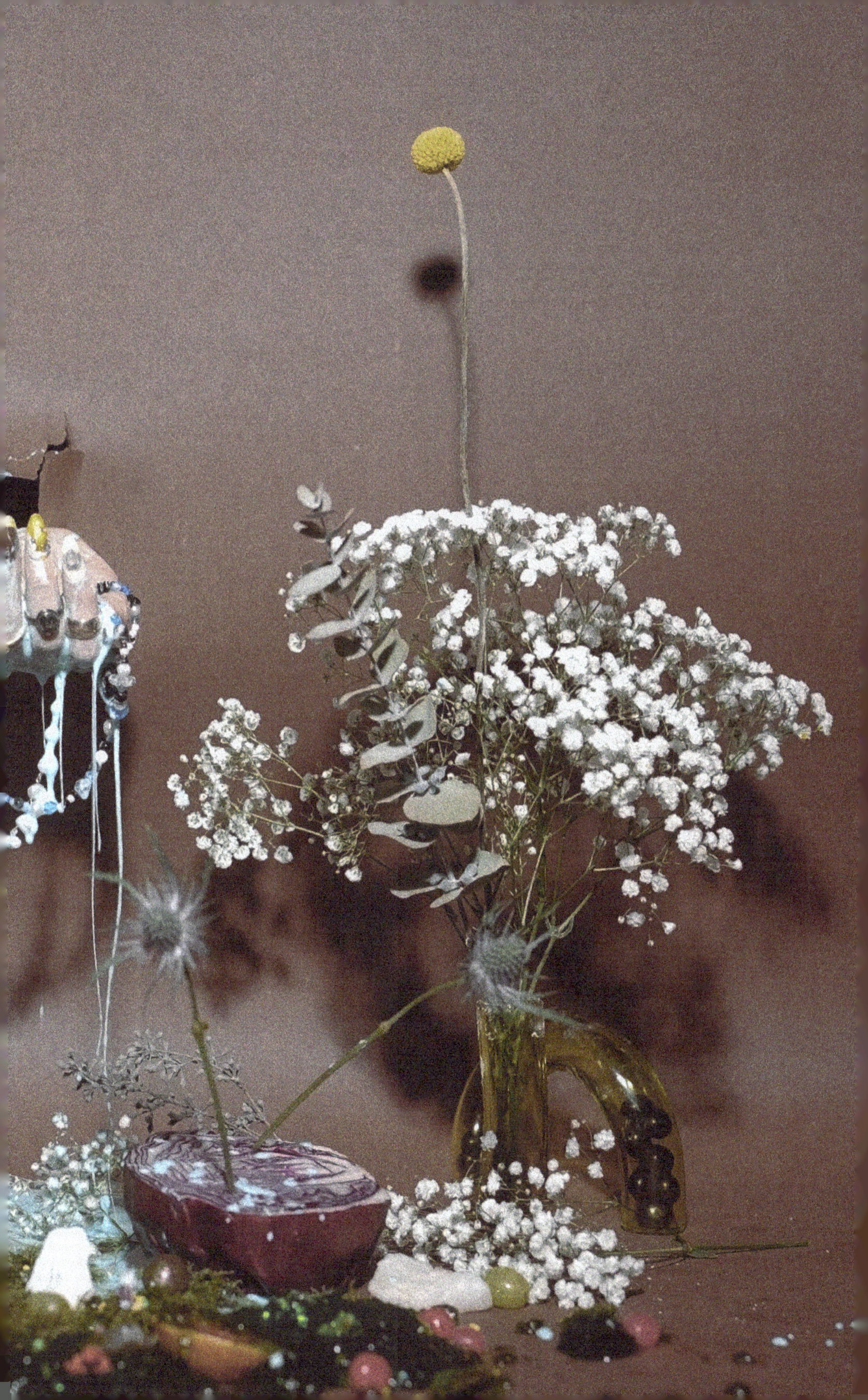

# SUCH GOL

Excerpt from an in-progress novel
by Dustin Hendrick

DEN

HOURS

The letter informing Darby of his mother's looming death had been delivered to the financial office of his studio, where it sat in a to-be-read pile for at least a week before it found him on the other side of the sprawling lot where he starred in his next role, a hastily written detective drama that would go nowhere and captivate no one. The letter's author was a well-intentioned woman, a member of the church in some capacity, who'd been tasked with caring for the rapidly declining Abigail in her final days. This woman knew nothing of Darby and his mother, that they had not spoken in nearly a decade, that he'd ceased to call her mother even before he left home, or that her propensity for violence and cruelty sparked Darby's own in that final morning before he left her and North Dakota behind, and never once returned.

The birdlike face of the intern who delivered it bore the obvious guilt of having opened, read, and re-sealed the letter; which he couldn't blame her for, as he would've done the same thing if, in such a pile of letters, he'd come across one addressed to a star. He thanked the girl and sent her away. He read the letter again, and slid it into the pocket of his jacket. He could only assume that Abigail, by now, was already dead, and he was right, she was, and another letter would follow in a few days to confirm this. He waited to feel something, anything, as the makeup girl dabbed the beads of summer sweat from his neck and reapplied the powder to his face—guilt, loneliness, satisfaction, relief—but it didn't come, and his other name was called, his created name, they were ready for him, for Finn Howard. The mask had been applied, and he had work to do. His jacket, and the letter tucked inside it was whisked away by wardrobe forever.

That night, a party to celebrate the release and success of the film he'd completed the year prior, *The Lock and Key Boys*, for which the coastline of Mendocino County had been deemed by the studio a suitable substitute for the war-scarred shores of northern France. *The Lock and Key Boys* would be his cinematic peak in the eyes of whatever critics decide these things and etch them into the stones of history, though he wouldn't know it for many years. Darby's anxious face (Finn's face now, he reminds himself endlessly) suited the director's vision for the role of the priest tasked with comforting and consoling the doomed and soon-to-be-doomed. The priest would die, as most do in stories like this one, and that death would be hailed as a defining moment in the film that brought even the most stalwart of audience-goers to tears. *A strange thing*, he thinks, *to die over and over and be applauded for it. A strange way to keep the lights on.*

He chooses a dark suit, stony blue, never worn before, tailored not for Darby, but for Finn. The jacket boasts ornate brass buttons shaped like bloomed roses, and when he fastens it, he feels safe. As though the weak spot in his midsection is hidden, his soft underbelly no longer exposed to predators. He shaves his face clean and slicks his blond hair back with beeswax, all the while practicing Finn's smile, Finn's contemplative glower, Finn's look of pleasant surprise in the bathroom mirror. He says goodbye to Jane, eight months pregnant now, and sick for most of it. She barely looks up from her magazine in response, her expression a combination of absence and pain. Though she's beautiful even so, he thinks, her pale skin glowing, her red-brown hair thick and shining beneath the lamp. Darby feels something like guilt stir up inside himself as he pulls his hard leather shoes on, and he realizes that he feels it constantly now, but it doesn't stop him from leaving.

He drives himself to the party, down into the valley as the sun sets and wonders if he shouldn't have called a car, something silver and shiny, to arrive in style, but he doesn't know what kind of party this is, doesn't know what to expect. He watches the streets darken and the sun go pink against the horizon. On a long stretch of empty road that leads into the city, he sees the streetlights on either side of the highway blink to life all at once like tall, night-blooming flowers—a welcome or maybe a warning, and with confidence and trained charisma, Finn Howard takes the wheel. Darby feels himself fade, and he finds comfort in this, in Finn's presence, in Finn at last taking over. *Let him bear this burden,* Darby thinks. *Let the invented man be the real one, at least for tonight.*

The venue is smaller than he imagined—the elite back rooms of a larger club owned by one of the financiers. There's a well-stocked bar and a raised stage for performances, around which tables are filled with industry professionals in various states of dress, some men in starched suits, some in plain clothes, some women in glittering sheer dresses, some in finery so gaudy it could only have been stolen from some set or another: hats with dyed-pink feathers, turbans, and one heavy-looking medallion on a gold chain he swears he remembers from a pirate film he worked on in those first few chaotic years. His table is the actors' table, and to his right sits Willie, the doomed but smiling pilot in the film, his dark skin seeming all the darker for the hanging smoke and low, overhead light. His teeth flash in the dim as he winks and downs his whiskey.

A stream of congratulators rushes around the table. He thanks them with Finn's voice. He smokes endless nervous cigarettes and drinks whiskey and soda and wine, the taste fading as the effect takes hold. And it helps him. The suit begins to fit, and so do the room, and the people. Finn glows brighter as the lights go liquid, as the smoke collects like a storm cloud against the ceiling.

The voices grow louder, giddier, a great throng of beings melding into one writhing, sparkling mass. Finn Howard approves. Abigail is most likely dead, Darby's mother dead, and Finn thinks *no matter, what did she ever matter,* and with Darby's long arm, Finn signals the floating man with the tray for another, *bring the bottle, he'll pay,* and the man brings it, no need to pay, and Willie laughs at the notion. *Don' you know where you're at?* Willie says, playful to a fault. Brilliant laugh, brilliant smile closing on a cigar in his perfect teeth. More whiskey. *Forget the soda now. Give it to me straight!* A voice in the back says, and the table laughs in agreement. A white cloth screen is wheeled up to the stage, and their film begins. Darby feels a shifting in the darkened room, sees Willie reaching across the table to snatch a full glass of wine. He drinks it down in one swift tilt, Darby watching the motion of his throat instead of watching himself, or a version of himself, onscreen.

*End,* the screen says, in gleaming white letters, and light, brighter even than before, blasts his table, the stars' table. Applause, and calls to stand, which Finn does. The screen is moved away and a short expensive-looking man takes its place, offering more praise: *a job well done indeed* he says, *now please enjoy: a special performance for a special cast and crew.*

More smoke now, artificial smoke, and a thrumming hint of music from the band behind the stage curtains. A woman appears, then three men emerge and crouch reverentially in front of her. The woman's skirts are long and watery, her dark blue top transparent, revealing a lithe form and a dark brazier over small breasts and strong arms—like Jane's. And

A *strange thing*, he thinks, *to* die over and over and be applauded for it. A strange way to keep the lights on.

he misses his wife, home and sleeping, soon to bring his child into the world, his tempestuous, magnificent, red-haired daughter. He wishes Jane was there with him, her strong limbs and cutting humor holding him down on the earth, an anchor and a shield.

The woman begins her dance, slowly raising a blue shawl with a gemmed embroidery of flowers that catch and reflect every bit of light remaining in the room. Darby looks at Willie looking at her, and Willie's dark eyes find him and shine back in response, his lips curve upward in the beginnings of a grin, and he seems like the happiest man to ever walk the earth.

The crouching men rise now, toned arms and chests exposed in sleeveless red vests. The woman spins and writhes around them, made of silk and smoke and shadow. And then Darby understands the theme of the performance as the three men theatrically size each other up, then turn that same threatened gaze to the men in the audience, to Finn, watching from his table.

The music grows louder and the woman's dance grows more fervent in response. She sings a haunting tune in a high vibrato that her pursuers match in deep voices that rattle Darby's eardrums, so loud he imagines them being heard outside on the street, over the sound of the passing cars to the curious delight of passersby. Another whiskey. Another. A long hit of something from a little metal pipe that tastes like a woman's perfume— the last thing he recalls the flavor of that night. His heart beating, maybe too fast, but in rhythm with the drumming that seems to change the flow of time in that room, to twist it. The woman winds her way to his table, her hair soft on his shoulder, her hands taking his, both of hers the size of one of his own. *Come with me.*

Darby reels, the room is a carousel, and in this moment, confident Finn is nowhere to be seen. *No, no, please, no thanks*, he says, and a garish voice from somewhere in the club says *a married man, a faithful one, too* in a tone of either disappointment or mockery. But the woman in blue has no time for this, and she moves on to Willie, who leaps up from the table with glee and shouts *I'll handle this* to cheers of approval, and the same voice from the back says *now here's a real man, if a colored one*, and as Willie hands Darby his glass Darby feels a syrup of stinging jealousy rise in his throat. He washes it down with the mouthful of tasteless whiskey left in Willie's glass, an electric pulse of pleasure taken in the fact that Willie's mouth had only moments before rested on the rim of that glass where his own now rest, the same pour of whiskey inside both of them.

Willie dances to his own disjointed beat, glorious and childlike, as the woman keeps perfect time with the band. Darby traces the movement of his body. Through the haze he sees Willie watching him as he dances, his eyes fixed on Darby's. Or is it Finn's? He'll never truly know. The woman's form ripples as she spins past, and she becomes Jane, dancing there in the center of that smoke-filled room, her belly flat, the swell of their child missing from this conjured version of her, Jane as she was when they met, on that film in the desert, his rodeo queen, her height a match for his own, eyes sharp and full, her rust-colored hair long and loose like the dancing woman's, and Willie next to her, just as beautiful as Jane, just as overwhelming, and he thinks: *Can I do it? Can I love them both?*

And he does.

Realization strikes like a fist, and he feels himself slipping, letting go, transforming, no going back now, not now that he knows, not now that his love is on display. He grips the leg of the table beneath the black cloth, *steady man, hold on, no one knows, hold on.* And in the whirl of that crowded room, in that lightning strike of clarity, as the scene careens toward some great end, he sees, standing calmly in a dim unoccupied corner, his mother, Abigail, arms folded, surely dead, all fixed up like she used to be, in the good days when Joe was still alive and she was still alive, really alive, before she gave up on him and on herself, her hair pulled back and up, a bit too severe but somehow still beautiful to the child he once was.

Calmly, with something akin to love she watches him, this man who was once her son. No smile, but a glint in those blue eyes, steel blue, those eyes he did not inherit. Yes, something like love.

The moment slows. He feels it grind against time, against those invisible, unstoppable gears—*mama, wait*, a child inside him says, maybe out loud this time, but drowned in the smoky tide of the room. The song's climax passes, and the dancing too, in turn begins to dwindle. A single long blink, don't let them see the tears he's too afraid to brush away, don't attract, for one moment don't draw attention, and Abigail is gone.

The song ends, abrupt, one final thick boom of the drum, a final rattle of the chimes from the blue woman. Willie seats himself with dramatized exhaustion to a raucous blast of applause, and they're closer this time, his thigh pressing against Darby's. He feels Willie's hand rest for a moment on his leg and he nearly weeps. He grabs Willie's hand with his own. *Don't stop*, that hand says, his heart all caught up in his throat, and the room shifts again. Willie makes no move, and his face betrays nothing, but something has given way here, something has stopped or began, he can't tell, but it's done now, and the spell of the dancing woman has faded, and there he is, starving for this other man.

Calls to stand, more applause, all around this time. *Such talent all around.* Darby and Willie linger in their seats, unseen for that one moment, and Willie's fingers press into the flesh just above Darby's knee, almost painfully. And then the hand is removed, and Darby's as well falls away from Willie's leg. Willie stands, and Darby does too, dragged from his seat by Finn, at the wheel and smiling humbly, grateful hand on lapel, *you're all too kind, thank you, so kind.* Willie's arm hooks around his shoulder and Darby nearly collapses against him. And again, the clasp of the hand, slightly too long, too firm, and then it's gone, yet Darby feels it still, years and years since, so many events of that night obscured in the haze of spirits and smoke and blinding light, but Willie's hands on him, pressing into him, asking the silent question, responding to Darby's own, those he has never forgotten.

He knows that this life is temporary, that it cannot last; that, in some way, it will escape him, that Darby Stachowicz will have no choice but to move on someday and leave Finn Howard behind. He knows this. He knows that Finn is in control now, that they've traded places, that this persona is now the great man of talent who is seen, who wants to be seen, and that Darby is nothing more than figment.

*It's enough*, he tells himself. *It has to be. It's what you asked for. It's inevitable.* And he loves it all, the lights, the praise, men and women wanting him, wanting Finn, wanting to be him. He wants it too, and the wanting soaks all through him down to the bones, so deep it frightens him.

His car speeds down the road to home.

He laughs—hollow, metallic, the sound quickly swallowed by the wind.

He knows it'll never be enough.

# THE INSTI OF

Adapted from an in-progress memoir
by Sara Atwood

# TUTE LIVING

Collage by Kimberlee Frederick

Summer 1990. While New England steams humidly and other sixteen-year-olds work summer jobs and cool off at the lake or the shore, I spend my weekdays driving 35 miles to Hartford, Connecticut every morning and the same distance home at night as an outpatient at The Institute of Living (formerly the Hartford Retreat for the Insane). After two years as a hunger artist, one hospital admission (at 81 pounds), months of failed therapy sessions, and a seemingly endless progression of bleak, despairing days, I've finally decided to reach for a lifeline.

These have been hard to come by. Mental health is not something people talk about in the early 90s; my 'condition' is the skeleton in the room, there is no Mental Health Awareness Month, no assemblies on stress or depression, certainly no Eating Disorders Awareness Week, or a National Eating Disorders Association to sponsor one (the American Anorexia and Bulimia Association, founded in 1978, offers a telephone hotline and chapters in many cities, but my parents have not heard about this, and no one recommends it). My Catholic high school employs guidance counselors, but their job is academic advisement, not therapy. The school's medical staff extends to an elderly nurse and nurse's aide, whose primary job is to tend fevers, nausea, cuts, and bruises. The theology department might be expected to take up the slack and minister to adolescent angst and worse, but its purpose is also academic.

The latest eating disorder research and the few mainstream books about anorexia aren't on my parents' radar. Like most people in our small New England town, my family doesn't have a home computer, and even if we did, there is no internet, no Google Scholar, no online support groups, no websites offering educational materials, assessments, providers' contacts, links to short films and TED talks. Anorexia is still often trivialized as 'the Slimmers' Disease,' an extreme exercise in vanity. My parents know a couple whose daughter is anorexic, but they've had the same trouble finding adequate information and the doctors they've dealt with (like our family physician and the psychiatrists they've referred us to), seem to know very little about the disease or treatment options. My mother learned of The Institute's program not from our family doctor but via a radio ad heard only by chance.

Set on thirty-five acres close to the center of Hartford, The Institute looks a lot like a university campus: well-appointed buildings set amid green lawns, winding walkways, and clusters of trees. Some of the structures date from the nineteenth century, such as the graceful, whitewashed building at the front of the campus. These are surrounded by newer, mostly brick buildings, although a few have been constructed in imitation wattle and daub. The quiet, parklike surroundings (designed by Frederick Law Olmsted) and collegiate character of the place make it



*I dug deep, but it was*
*rotten all the way down*

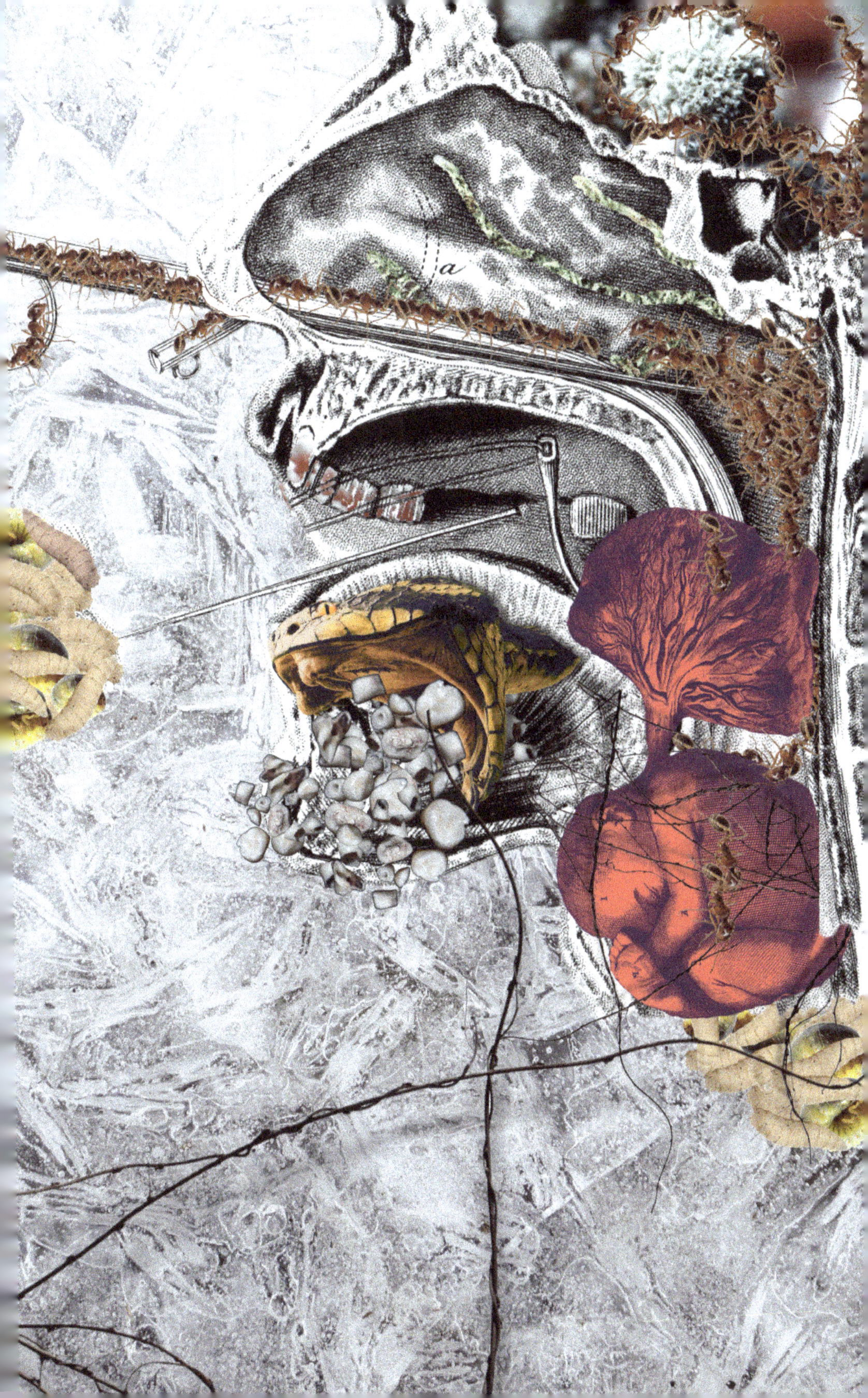
a

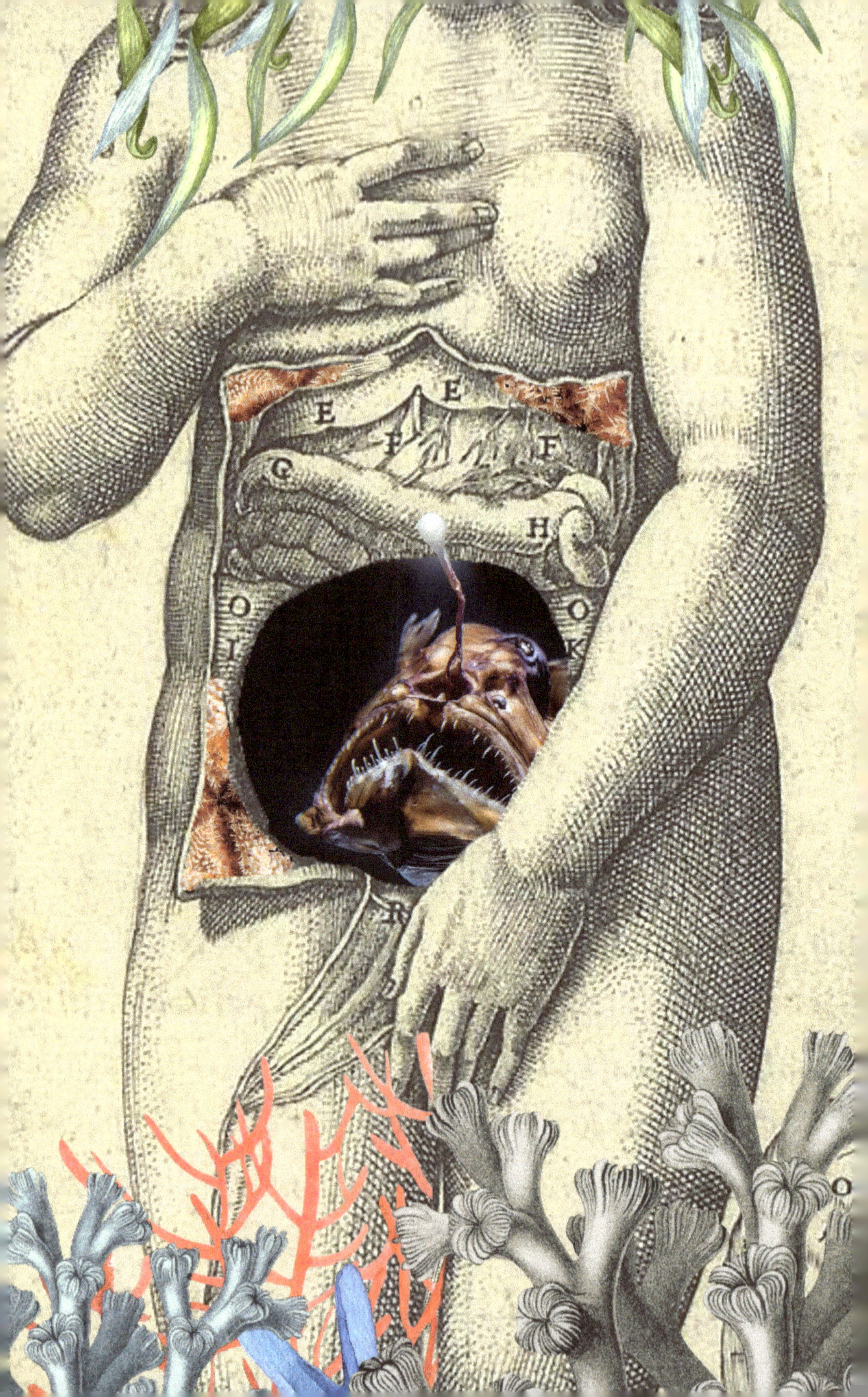

E
E
F
G
H
O
K
I
R
O

easy to forget that The Institute of Living is a psychiatric hospital.

There are only three other patients in the program this summer, all women, of different ages and backgrounds. I am the youngest. Sadie, dark-haired and olive-skinned, is in her forties, I think, though it's hard to tell: a long, dark ponytail combined with severe emaciation gives her the appearance of an ancient child. She has suffered from anorexia for years and been in and out of treatment; recently she was diagnosed with a brain tumor, which will likely kill her unless starvation does first. Sadie is a career anorexic; the disease is so much a part of her identity that it has become her default mode, her way of existing in the world. She hoards it as one would a treasure and betrays the anorexic's sly pride with her own extremity. I wonder what she was like when she was younger, before illness altered her body and mind. Sadie doesn't pretend to want to get better and often makes the therapists anxious by describing the satisfactions of restriction, which they don't want the rest of us to hear. She seems to derive mischievous pleasure in making them scramble to redirect her.

Rue is in her twenties, slender and attractive, with shoulder-length, almost-blonde hair and blue-gray eyes. Her weight is stable now, so you wouldn't know to look at her that she's both anorexic and bulimic. She's the one who interests me most, being closest to my age. She's spiky and cool, wears long skirts, and smokes cigarettes during our breaks. I'm intrigued by her worldliness, her long-limbed elegance, and a hint of recklessness and unpredictability. I sense some wound that has left her careless of consequences and of herself; her demons trail her, rustling their wings. One day during a break she tells us matter-of-factly that she was raped a few years ago and that she has tried to kill herself. I'm shocked by this information and for a brief, shameful moment I wonder whether her story is true; in my naïve, sheltered experience I've never (consciously) known anyone to whom these things have happened, and it seems impossible that the girl in front of me, calmly blowing smoke from between her lips, could have suffered such terrible experiences. How little I know about the world or about the proximity of violence, how it crouches, shapeshifting and inchoate, at the edges of the ordinary. Rue is little more committed to recovery than Sadie, but better able to pass, to mingle undetected among the well. I wonder what keeps her from just walking off The Institute's manicured grounds, hopping a bus to Boston or New York, and losing herself in some sort of precarious bohemian existence.

> How little I know about the world or about the proximity of violence, how it crouches, shapeshifting and inchoate, at the edges of the ordinary.

Terry is the odd one out in that she suffers from binge eating. Middle-aged, plump, with short dark hair, she wears a perpetually querulous expression. It's clear she feels at a disadvantage among women adept at starvation. She knows she's being judged and feels that the three of us don't understand her problem. She isn't wrong. Unable to see any parallels between her behavior and mine, I'm alarmed by what I consider her lack of self-control, her mindless gorging; I'm still telling myself that self-starvation is a *form* of control. What I don't recognize, and won't for years to come, is the affinity between all types of eating disorders, restrictive and otherwise—their common origin in self-disgust and trauma. Terry is using food as a language to express many of the same things as Sadie, Rue, and me; she's just speaking a different dialect. Many mental health and medical professionals don't recognize this yet either; binge eating won't be given its own designation until 2013, in the DSM-V. Her condition *is* poorly understood, even among the professionals, never mind the general public. It's a measure of The Institute's progressiveness that it recognizes binge eating as belonging on the spectrum of eating disorders and employs therapists trained in its treatment. Here at The Institute, Terry's behavior is acknowledged and taken seriously. Still, it can't be easy to be thrown together with the three of us.

We are overseen by a team: Amy, a dance and movement therapist, and Jill, an eating disorders therapist, are with us every day; Maureen, a nutritionist, plans our meals; two psychiatrists, Drs. Stuart and Hilton, meet with each of us weekly for individual sessions. I'm not sure what to make of these doctors. Though they seem old to me, they're probably only in their early forties. Dr. Stuart is slim and petite, with a carefully arranged blonde pageboy that hugs her face. She wears skirts, tailored blouses, and serviceable heels. Her manner is kind, but she maintains a clinical distance, cool and unreadable. I haven't had a female therapist before and she seems so put together I feel ugly beside her, painfully aware of my patient status. I'm embarrassed to be meeting her in my 'condition.' Dr. Hilton, on the other hand, is what I have come to think of as standard-issue male psychiatrist: small, wan body bundled into bland trousers and suitcoat, pale, watery eyes blinking nervously behind steel-framed glasses, soft white hands resting limply on desks or knees. Socially awkward and remote, he seems to me the same make and model as the other male psychiatrists I've seen, a sort of robo-shrink, programmed to decide my fate. Even though I've chosen to enter this program I'm still unwilling to talk about myself or my family with strangers, afraid that anything I say will be misconstrued, made to fit a preexisting diagnostic narrative. I haven't forgotten the narrowly-missed psych ward admission recommended by a previous therapist. Of course, the doctors may misread my reticence—what dark secrets is she hiding?—but whatever they imagine into my silence will say more about them than it will about me. I've wound myself up tightly, leaving no threads for them to pull on.

> ...he seems to me the same make and model as the other male psychiatrists I've seen, a sort of robo-shrink, programmed to decide my fate.

I'd like to offer a scene here, recreate a therapeutic interaction, but I gave so little away in those long-ago Institute sessions that I have no memory of what we spoke about. I offer an image instead: a nondescript office, functional carpet, potted plant, filing cabinets, a few unmemorable pictures. Dr. Hilton sits behind a wooden desk, glancing from the chart in his hands to where I sit in a chair across from him, just outside a shaft of late afternoon sun. As usual, he seems ill at ease; I'm vaguely pleased to think my silence may be the cause. I feel no rapport with him, no point of connection. He seems the sort of doctor more comfortable with textbooks than troubled teens. I can't imagine what he could know or understand about my life. The wall clock behind me ticks loudly in the silence. Dr. Hilton poses a question, adjusts his glasses. I blink back at him, briefly respond. What has he asked? How have I responded? I imagine myself quietly glimmering with Blakean flames:

The Human Dress, is forged Iron
The Human Form, a fiery Forge.
The Human Face, a Furnace seal'd
The Human Heart, its hungry Gorge.[1]

Our days in the program are divided into treatment blocks: group discussion, dance/movement, nature walks, food encounters. I enjoy being in the leafy, campus-like grounds and feel less like a patient outside. Dance therapy, on the other hand, activates my inhibitions. It feels foolish to stand in a group circle and put my body through a series of movements and poses. I'm certain I look awkward (I know the others do), and it all seems suspiciously 'New Age' to me. We're like a troop of sickly flower children, a gathering of scrawny charismatics. Dancing at an actual dance makes sense to me (although even then I'm self-conscious), but this just seems absurd. I'm not sure what sort of enlightenment I'm supposed to get from therapeutic movement. All I get is intensely uncomfortable.

Amy has explained that movement therapy is meant to reactivate the mind-body connection and foster emotional awareness. Eating disorder patients, she says, tend to dissociate from their bodies, which they perceive as shameful and disgusting; the body becomes the enemy. At the same time, ED patients numb themselves to emotion and sensation. The result is profound alienation, a sort of

*disembodiment.* Movement sessions are meant to help us reinhabit our bodies and relearn how to feel and express emotion. The idea is to become comfortable with and in our bodies, to become a fully integrated person. All this touchy-feely stuff makes me cringe.

At our movement sessions, Amy pushes the chairs back against the wall and instructs us to form a circle on the brown carpet in the center of the room. She shows us how to loosen our limbs to dispel muscular tension. I feel acutely embarrassed as she bends and sways, moving her arms in sweeping motions. She looks silly: a middle-aged, mid-sized woman gliding around a bland institutional space. Sadie and Rue are as reluctant to join in as I am. Terry, trying to impress Amy and separate herself from the mad fasting girls, swishes her arms around, smiling determinedly. It all feels inane, like a cross between a hippie 'love-in' and kindergarten circle time.

Rue, Sadie, and I stand self-consciously, making halfhearted gestures with our hands and shuffling our feet.

"Come on ladies," Amy urges, "make an effort. Try to feel the pleasure of the movement, tune into your bodies."

Rue flashes me a "Does she believe this crap?" look. I sigh and give a half-hearted sway.

Amy begins walking around to each of us, gently lifting our arms into position. "Don't think about it, just experience it. Can you remember a moment when your mind and your body were one, when you felt completely present and focused?"

More mumbo jumbo, I think, resisting the urge to shake Amy's hand from my shoulder. But something is nagging at me. I *do* remember a moment—moments—like that. It's how I feel when I run: moving swiftly, everything distilled down to the rhythm of my breath, the cadence of my footfalls, the steady beat of my heart. Those moments when I am coextensive with the road, the earth, the sky, senses

[1] *William Blake, "A Divine Image" (1794), Songs of Innocence and Experience*

hyperalert to the wind, the scent of fallen leaves, the sting of rain. The feeling of being not just in but *of* the world. A feeling I've keenly missed since my doctor declared me too fragile to continue running. Now, for a fleeting second the sensation returns, lighting up my nerve endings and lifting me away from the dull room, the awkward circle. When it goes, I could cry.

I let Amy lift my skinny arms, palms turned upwards, and now the gesture is a supplication: *let me have that feeling back again. I want it back.*

We eat all three meals at the program: breakfast upon arrival, lunch at midday, an afternoon snack, and dinner just before we go home. These meals are a source of considerable anxiety for all four of us. I am panicked by the thought of eating so much food in one day; of having no involvement in choosing or preparing it; and of eating in company and under the watchful eyes of therapists who know all the tricks (napkins must remain open and above the table here, for instance, and because some of our number are known to purge, we are expected to use the bathroom before meals, not during or shortly after). I'm here by choice, sure, and I want to get better, but doing so isn't like stepping nimbly from one rock to another across a placid stream, it's like leaping a torrent, and at this point, I'm still clinging to the shore. There's safety in ritual—counting calories, checking my weight, eating on a rigid schedule—without it I'm untethered and likely to be swept away.

The therapists know all this, of course, and the meals are a critical part of treatment, intended not only to provide balanced nutrition but also to gradually restore a healthy relationship with food. Interaction with the cooks encourages us to take interest in food preparation and to see that cooking can be pleasant and creative. Communal meals are meant to reintroduce us to eating as a shared, social experience, a source of satisfaction rather than shame. They also provide an opportunity to address triggers as they arise. Here in the program, we can confront our fear and disgust in a safe environment, with professional and peer support: if Sadie feels unable to eat her bread, we can reassure and encourage her; if Terry still feels unsatisfied and empty after finishing a meal, we can help her try to understand why (that's the idea, at least; the three of us would struggle to help her with this). The thinking is that by doing so, with therapeutic guidance, we will develop skills with which to face our anxieties and change our behavior. Although I don't know it at this point, this is fairly standard Cognitive Behavioral Therapy (CBT), an approach aimed at teaching people to confront what they fear, learn healthier ways of coping and productively alter thinking and behavior. Thirty years on, after seeking help for a loved one through Dialectical Behavioral Therapy (DBT), a modified form of CBT, I'll learn that the founder of DBT, Dr. Marsha Linehan, was admitted to The Institute of Living at age 17 in 1961. Suicidal, severely depressed, and often violent, she remained hospitalized at The Institute for 26 months.

Though they loom so large for us, the meals themselves are objectively unexceptional. The regular dining schedule appeals to ED patients' need for predictability and routine, creating a sense of safety amidst alarming challenges. While coercion is never used or condoned, we are all expected to eat our meals without complaint or resistance. I am not yet a vegetarian, which is probably a good thing because alternative diets of any kind are considered suspect; many eating disorder patients use them to enable restriction. Exceptions are made for legitimate, documented food allergies, but that's all; none of the therapists here wants to hear

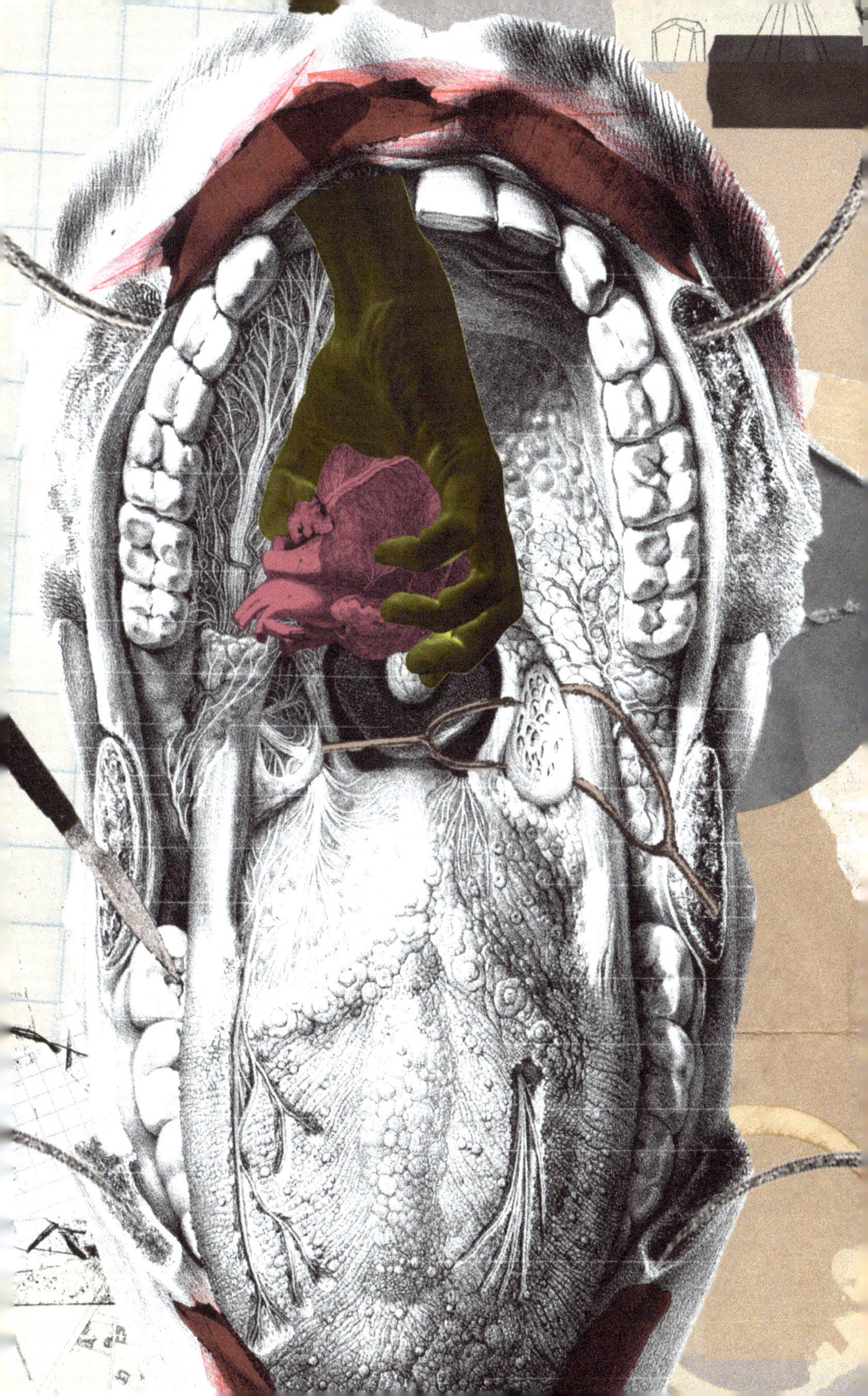

about food preferences or aversions. The point is to learn how to eat again, without prejudice; there are no 'good' or 'bad' foods here at The Institute.

Breakfast, eaten just after we arrive for the day, is what healthy people would call light: fruit and yogurt, eggs, toast. Lunch might be hot or cold, depending on the day—various salads, sandwiches, soups—and dinner is usually meat/fish paired with a starch and vegetable, along with bread. Snacks might consist of fruit, yogurt, cheese, nuts. The food is nutritious, simple, and generally well-prepared. Most of it tastes alright, if a bit bland. To me, it just feels like way too much food. Since my hospital stay over a year ago, I've managed to keep my weight at something just north of perilous, but my idea of a regular meal is still skewed and I'm used to being able to indulge my preferences and aversions, to eat the same 'safe' foods every day in the same, ritualized way. My parents just want me to eat, so they don't fuss much anymore when they see me methodically paring paper-thin slices from an apple and eating them off the knife, slowly nibbling at a bowl of dry cereal, counting the number of times I chew each bite of food. But that sort of thing won't fly here. Not only are the meals much too close together for me, there's also a mid-morning and mid-afternoon snack. I like to put many hours between meals so that I can achieve a feeling of emptiness before having to eat again. Under this new regime, I often feel gorged after eating and struggle with self-disgust, especially in the early days of the program.

One day about midway through the program, I'm confronted with a dish of canned beets. I've never laid eyes on a beet before, much less tasted one, so I've no idea what to expect. When the beets appear at our evening meal, I'm misled by their appearance. They are aesthetically cunning: the deep purplish color of the flesh and the stewing juices suggest sweetness—calling to mind berries, plums, sangria, jam. The bite-sized pieces of beet look like magenta chunks of honeydew or pear, soft and finely-textured. Primed by these associations, my brain is unprepared for the sour, earthy taste and slippery-solid substance of the actual beets. ("The beet was Rasputin's favorite vegetable," writes Tom Robbins, "You could see it in his eyes"). The first misgivings come as my fork passes under my nose, trailing a distinctly unpleasant smell, but then the beet is in my mouth and I'm grimacing, gagging, narrowly resisting the urge to spit it out. I swallow with difficulty and my gorge rises as I look at the still-full dish.



Amy is watching me calmly. "Everything alright?" she asks, "Have a drink of water."

I reach for my glass and take a big gulp, washing the taste down, but it lingers.

"I don't think I can eat these," I say. "I've never had them before, and I really don't like them."

Amy eyes me skeptically. "They're just beets," she says, "and they're the vegetable tonight." Does she think my revulsion is a bit of anorectic playacting, that I have some disease-induced beet vendetta?

I look back at the dish, the chunks glistening in the rancid liquid, sanguine and nasty. I can't imagine taking even one more bite. Desperately, I try to bargain.

"I'll eat a different vegetable," I promise Amy hopefully, "whatever you like. I just can't eat these." Then, stupidly, "They make me feel like I'm going to throw up."

I mean this literally—the beets trigger my gag reflex—but I've spoken rashly, unthinkingly invoking a behavior common to ED patients. Talking about throwing up in an eating disorders program is like mentioning a bender at AA. ("Rashness," Virginia Woolf says, "is one of the properties of illness").

Amy sits back in her chair with a kind but firm expression on her face. Rue, Sadie, and Terry have gone quiet, awaiting the outcome of this contest. There's an aspect of suspended animation to the scene, as though the room itself is holding its breath. A flicker of tension licks the air.

"I'm sorry you don't like the way they taste," Amy says evenly, "but you know we don't offer substitutions. They're part of tonight's meal and we're all having them. Sometimes there will be foods served here that you or others don't like, but it's important to eat them and find out that nothing terrible happens."

No way is she going to negotiate. I can tell from her tone that this conversation is closed. My stomach sinks, then lurches. I could make a fuss, but I don't like conflict and anyway, it probably wouldn't change the outcome: *I'm going to have to eat these beets.* I usually like Amy well enough but right now I hate her with a force that surprises me. Her manner is reasonable and resolved rather than authoritarian, but I feel like a helpless child—or worse, like what I am: a patient. Everyone else waits to see whether I'll rebel (what would happen then?) or relent. I imagine screaming at Amy, overturning the damn dish, storming out of the dining room. I pick up my fork, glare at her, and spear another bite of beet. The room relaxes, conversation resumes. Amy looks as if she wants to say something more, but instead gives me a nod of encouragement and turns to talk to Sadie. I sit silently, choking down the beets and chasing each bite with water. After three or four minutes that feel like hours, the dish is empty.

Amy turns to me. "What are you feeling right now?" she asks, her eyes searching my face. I stare stonily back at her, saying nothing, full with beets and outrage.

At home that night I recount the story to my mother, who is torn between supporting the program and her sympathy for me (it turns out she doesn't like beets either, which explains their previous absence from my life). Later, I lie in bed stewing in my own sour juices. All this time I've been cooperative and compliant; I've toed the program's line. What was the point of making me eat something that turns my stomach? I lie there steaming, pressure rising. Vesuvius at home.

As I stare at the ceiling, thrumming with anger, I realize I'm completely present, completely focused and though this isn't the sort of pleasant, Zen-like embodiment that we're aiming at in movement therapy, it's no less clarifying. Suddenly it occurs to me that maybe *this* was the point. Amy could have given me a pass, but she'd pushed me, pressured me. Had she meant to prod me out of my careful self-containment? *How do you feel right now?* she'd asked me, and I'd refused to answer. But I am feeling more than I've felt in ages.

# DEE

Fiction by Noelle Smith

# PER

Printmaking by Claire Gunville

y roommate's fish tank has entered my subconscious. Two things to know before I get into it:

> 1. It's a stretch to call me a roommate. Crashing-friend is more on the money… I'm in between jobs. I just moved to this city. She's kind enough to let me hang around to feed the fish and water the plants while she's out of town.
> 2. I'm a serial plant-killer. I'm working on it. I want to change.

It was the night before she left. We stayed out late and got whiskey-drunk as you do before an early airport trip. We spoke loudly to each other at the bar about all the men we let mess with us in our twenties. It was cathartic. We stumbled back to her living room and sank into the couch side by side. I hadn't paid much attention to the fish tank before, but the otherwise darkened room snapped my attention to its aqueous glow. We sat in silence before the pulsing interplay of aquatic forces.

The biggest fish wheeled around freely in the center of the tank, its mouth popping open intermittently on bony hinges. Its eyes unblinking as portholes. When Big Fish moved it sent the rest of the tank swirling away like a lava lamp blob governed by gradual convection.

Above Big Fish was the fast-moving school of medium-sized fish that darted just below the surface (I called them the piranhas jokingly because they nipped your fingers). At the very bottom of the tank, hidden amongst the rocks, were the tiniest minnows of the bunch. I pondered my soon-to-be charges for a while in an inebriated trance.

"I see why you got into fish," I say, mesmerized.

As I observed, the aquarium revealed itself to be a system propelled by a brutal natural order. It wasn't a constant feeding frenzy simply because the smallest fish were just fast enough to get out of the way. Everyone was equipped with what they needed to survive if they were diligent and kept swimming. It looked tiring. I couldn't help but associate the whole thing with the human dynamics we'd just been discussing at the bar. Late-night considerations of samsara, existence, reincarnation…

Yeah, I've done a psychedelic or two in my day like every self-respecting adult, so what? I would say it loosened my mind from default human-world fixations. I can soft-gaze away from the surface level of things at my leisure when I get bored. I can get lost in some truly far-out stuff if I'm not careful.

I'd seen this dance before on Animal Planet. This little number is called "Who can I fit in my mouth." The ocean-dwellers know it well. Their very being is a streamlined digestive track. They approach life mouth first, suspended in water like a blade. They swim around gobbling down other entities whole until one day something larger comes up quickly from behind and *CHOMP*.

Here's something I heard again recently, bringing a middle-school biology lesson back like a surge of hormonal acne and bad haircuts:

Humans, like fish, and all other vertebrates begin their life as an asshole. The cluster of embryonic cells forms a dent which deepens to become an early gut. The gut works its way to the other side, eventually becoming the mouth. This makes a tube. Our type of life starts out anus first. We're what we call deuterostomes.

1. I remind myself of this when I start to feel special.
2. We build ourselves around hunger, first things first.
3. I had continued my descent into the fish tank.

My throat started swelling as I walked down the sidewalk a week later, out for a neighborhood jaunt. The more panicky I got, the more it tightened. I called my friend gasping but hung up after a few rings and decided to handle it privately. I didn't want to come off unhinged. Anxiety is normal in a situation like mine. Between jobs. New to a city. Alone.

I was sure that's all it was: anxiety, until I crawled onto the couch and began to sweat with a burgeoning fever. I was kind of relieved there was a reason behind the off feeling. Waves of delirium washed over my body. My immune system rallied its defenses and decided to fight with FIRE. I lay back by the light of the aquarium, sweating. The water gurgled through the filter in spurts and gasps. I was too ill to turn on the overhead light as the sun dipped out of the sky. There was a queasy brightening as the city darkened. It was coming from the tank. It radiated an uneasy gloom like a drowned lamp and washed the room in undulating sea-sick colors.

Over the next three days I got up to drink water, to pee, and to feed the fish.

Once upon a fever dream, the universe was cloudy water around a hot ocean vent. Deep-space angels with tentacles for arms combed the furnace—like liquid harps. And so music was invented.

Once upon a fever dream, the universe was cloudy water around a hot ocean vent. Deep-space angels with tentacles for arms combed the furnace–like liquid harps.

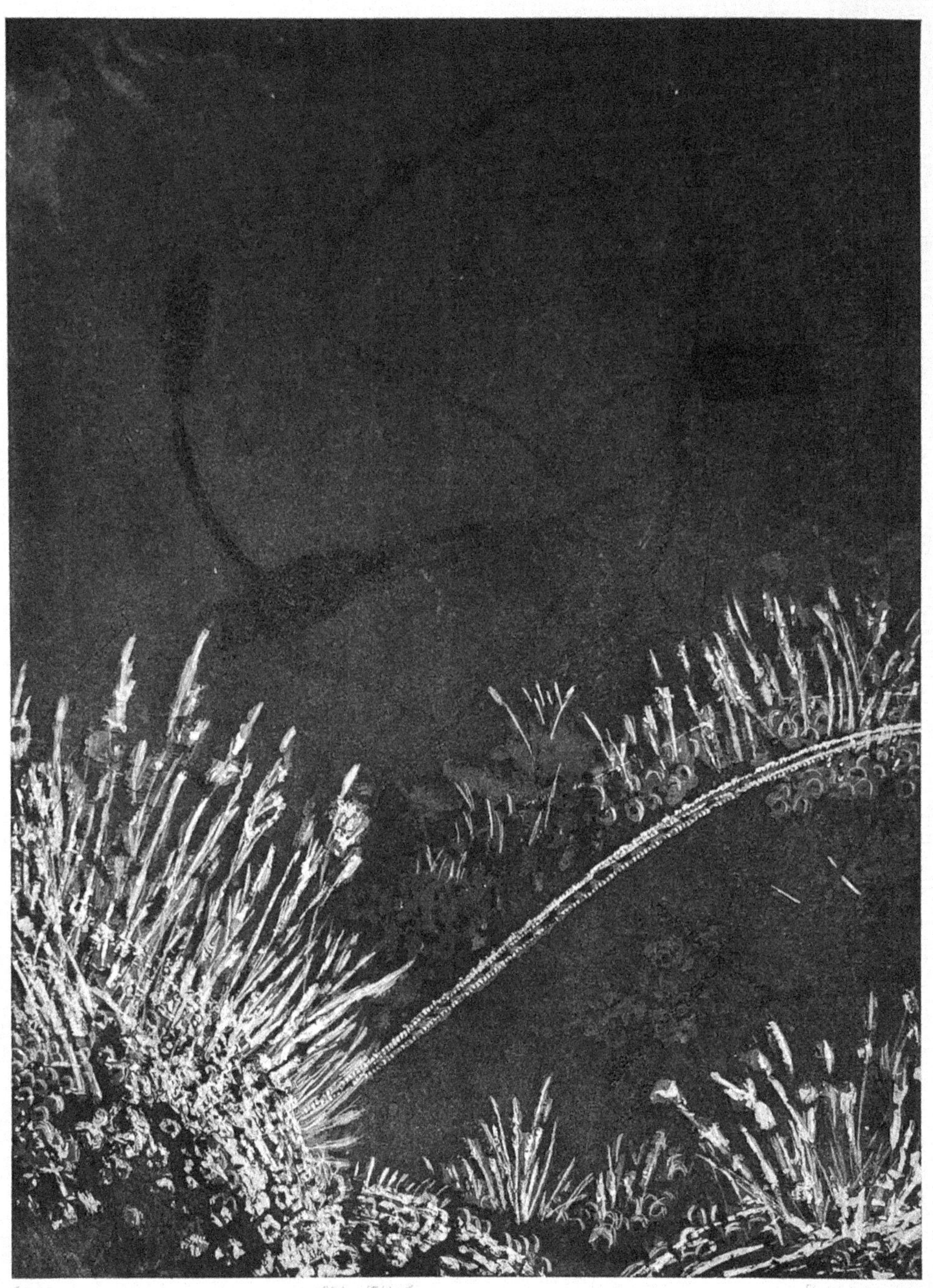

3/14
SEA FLOOR

I met an old man on a jetty who told me the sun is a glowing ball above the open jaws of an angler fish. "That's a story for a different depth," I tell him. "I'm only a monkey."

The pet hermit crab I kept as a teenager never felt the pull of tides or scuttled beneath a full moon and for that, I am truly sorry. Their lifespan is upwards of 30 years in the wild. They would have 15 years left if still alive. You can do a lot with 15 years.

When ships went down throughout history they never came back up. There were no deep-sea explorations, no cameras, no shipwreck tourists. The ocean could have been infinitely deep for all we could do about it. I bet an island populated by one beloved castaway lived in each widow's heart. Sometimes the unknowing is a buoy to hold onto, if you will. I'd like to believe in good endings, I'm not sure I can find another way to live.

One of the medium-sized fish jumped from the tank in the night. When I found him the next morning I studied his stiff little body. He looked like a sardine. "Just flush him down the toilet," my friend says on the phone. "I just keep the tank. They handle the politics."

Sometimes I wonder if the predators humans encounter nowadays don't have fins or teeth or eyes—maybe they are big bad ideas dark and nebulous and twice as greedy. Sticky as a glue trap. Caustic enough to dissolve a person slowly.

I've seen friends entangled in seagrass fighting to keep their heads above water. I wonder if I am that friend. It depends whose shore you're standing on.

The water isn't looking so good. I consider the possibility of an algae bloom.

Turns out I didn't clean it right. It's not that deep. The filter got messed up. I was sick. I'm prone to depression.

I go deeper. Turns out there are a lot of ways to avoid your life. I've tried out quite a few.

I prefer disassociation. Fish your wish. My subconscious gets green and slimy fast when I refuse to pay attention to it. I can see it reflected right in front of me in real-time. I wear glasses. I wasn't built to focus like a normal person. I can only see things right in front of my face.

What kind of asshole can't muster the attention span to clean a fish tank once a week? This kind, I guess. I'm a deuterostome like the rest of them. I assemble the energy and get my hands wet. I water the plants, suddenly aware of them. I'm not sure how many days have gone by. Was it one week or two? The fish tank gets clean and the energy in the whole apartment eases. I start to feel better. My appetite comes back.

I fix myself a sandwich built from other beings' bodies and settle on the couch in front of the fish tank. It's morning. I take a bite of their remaining parts, humming with pleasure.

I've opened the window. The sensation of stagnant air being sucked out feels good on my exposed skin. My limbs feel fresh and flexible. I appreciate my body returned to me. I chew my sandwich, molars grinding the processed grains. Incisors snapping rubbery meat. I lick mayo from my thumb.

It's like bodies are something hunger dreamed up to be held by. It's no good to be empty. We only are what we can hold inside of us, at least for a moment.

Before me, the fish tank whirls on like a contained universe. I've turned the lights off to suppress the algae bloom as instructed. Big Fish is looking a little bigger, now that I really look at him. He's got a distended paunchy belly sheathed in scales. He wags his whole body in the center of the dim tank, turning one flat eye toward me and then the other. Most of the time he looks indistinctly brown, but today his scales are as stripey as a tiger. Now that I look a little closer, half of the small fish are gone.

"I'm writing a story about your fish tank," I tell my friend over the phone, briefly outlining the gist of it.

"That's not how I view it at all," she says. "But that's *interesting.*"

The glass is kind of streaky, I notice. I'm feeling capable. I clean the glass with a rag and windex in brisk circular motions. If you gaze at the glass up close you can see your own watery reflection.

# A SPE

Poetry by Emily Moon

# CIAL

# CASE

Drawing by Megan Chin

i  am  s h e
    of the last minute
      filling every moment
          with    b u s y ness
              split by infinitives of
            sitting and thinking
          circular    thoughts
      that lead to lava
lamp mindscapes
    glitter bomb
        my attention
          with tiny shiny
              thought objects
            parallax processes
        bruise my brain
      slightly  s k e w
perception into a
    special case of oval
        an   akimbo   place
            where  tasks   are
              completed just in
                  t    i    m    e

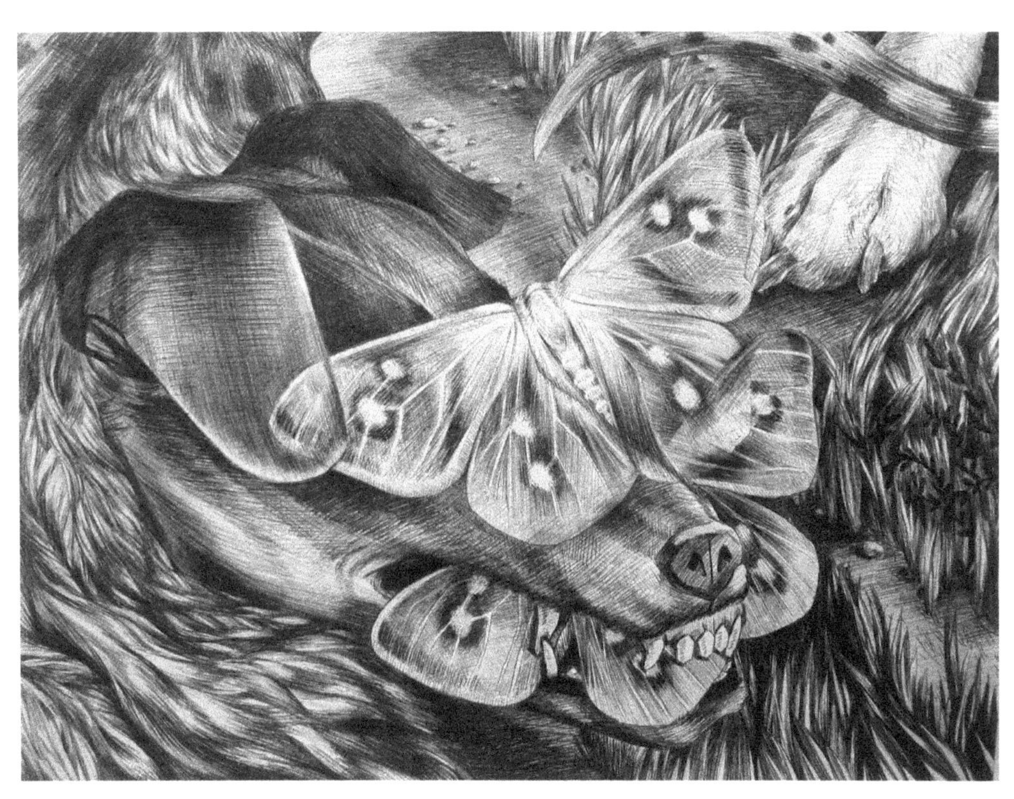

*Spirit in the Night*

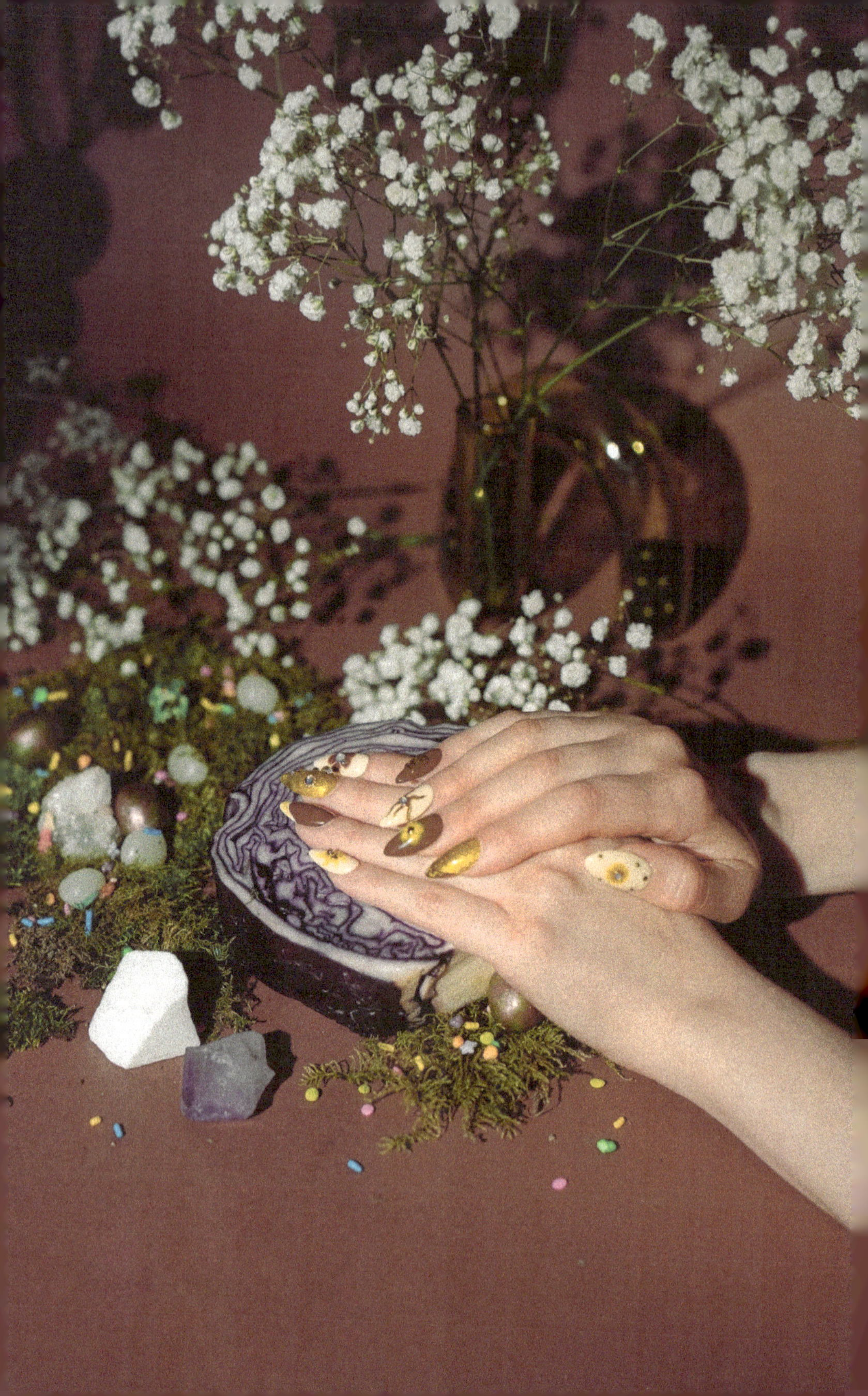

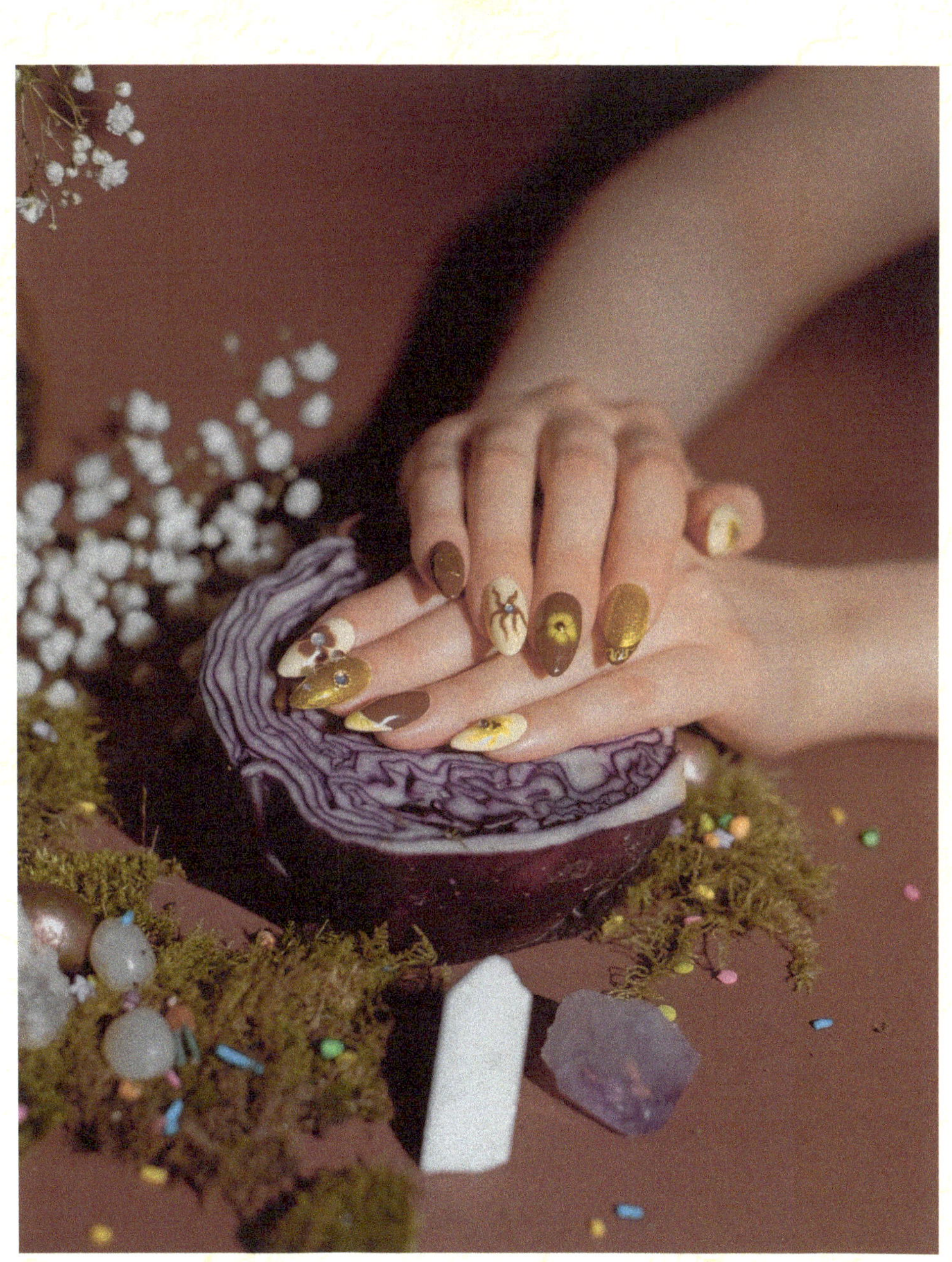

# TRANS

Creative Non-Fiction by Jack Wang

# PLANT

Photography by Judy Jiang

*ing not from the mountain high, but the valley pinched between two cliffs. The bottom of a canyon, where the shriek of a desert bird reverberates. Sing now from the bottom of Hemingway's iceberg.*

*I wanted to write a poem that would get me to the top of a mountain. I find valleys and streams festering with consciousness instead. I hadn't heard anything that wasn't an echo. Hadn't traveled far enough back to hear the origin of the sound. I wander on my knees, putting my ear to the earth, I hear trees growing from strange roots.*

My parents immigrated in 1990. My father left China—with Her language, food, and loved ones—behind. He would never see his own father again.

My mother followed him a year later. She cleaned bathrooms and watched children. Her big break was taking an analyst position with the Boston Police Department. She hated working there. Documenting the intricate details of homicide, domestic violence, and overdose.

She was one of a few hundred thousand Chinese raised Christian. She carried me to term for nine months and when she went into labor, she did so for 12 hours without an epidural.

When I was delivered, the doctor told my mother that my head size was in the 99th percentile. He also told her that I had a small hole in my heart wall. My mother wailed like my father did when he learned his father had passed—clutching a pay phone and a prepaid international calling card. Each second a nickel passing by.

My mother would cry again when she found cellophane wrappers full of pills in an old shoebox where only a few years earlier she'd tolerated swimsuit magazines.

I remember crying in a bathtub. The sterile smell of Johnson & Johnson's tear-free formula rubbed roughly on my face. The teardrop label promised a gentle wash but stung my eyes with a harsh chemical trace.

We moved west, to a new home in a Minnesota suburb. I light incense and bow three times before Guan Yin Pu Sa. I tune my guitar down a half-step like Jimi Hendrix and sand down the edges of a broken bottle neck like Robert Johnson.

In the wail of Jimi's guitar and Johnson's voice, I learned how to act out like a blues-man and mourn like a rockstar. You bend notes and break up lines to fill in the space. But when the shapes don't fit, a hole becomes a crack.

Fill your stomach. When I grew up, it was the feeling of an empty stomach I couldn't stand. My dad said over Thanksgiving dinner—a table set with bao and turkey. The yellow spot in his eye twitched like it might burst.

Fairy Tale Land 2

112

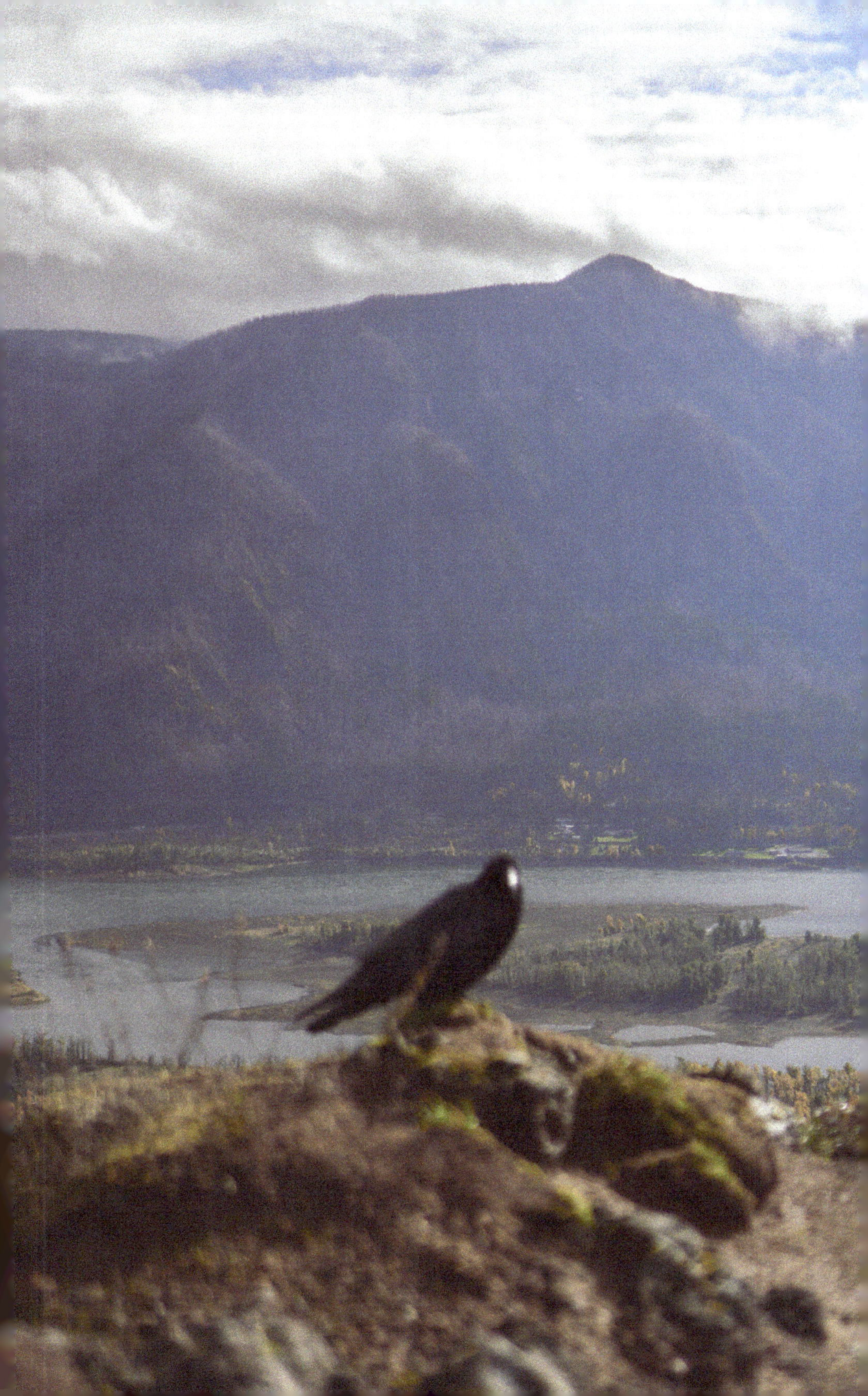

My dad could never have imagined what I'd find here. He dreamed of full bellies. What else could a kid want?

I wanted to fill my ears. The radio signal tuned the dial, told me to breathe in through my nose and again with my mouth. I crushed pills and mixed the white powder with alcohol to form a paste. I painted my gums and danced around a bonfire.

I danced my way into the back of a cop car. Stolen cigarettes burning a hole in the inside of a jacket pocket. The back of a patrol vehicle is small and plastic. There isn't enough room for your knees.

What could you expect of someone born with such a large head and a small hole in their heart? Would they not think of the worst ways to fill it?

I knew what the Invisible Man felt like. Who knew but that, on the lowest frequencies, Louis Armstrong played a Chinese horn? Art Warren wasn't as taken with the idea. Didn't particularly care for Ellison. Ralph wrote some music criticism, proselytizing the virtues of bebop, and Art couldn't overlook that.

Art played free jazz. He didn't go to college but stayed in the scene in Minneapolis. One time, Art stopped playing mid-show and started a fistfight with David King for relying too heavily on old rhythms. You said you wanted it free, so free it up, man!

In high school, Art was already an artist, playing shows and cooking spoons. He started a journal and wanted me to write for it. I didn't yet have any pretense. I wrote what I felt, branding a stream of slogans and song lyrics onto the page. Art thought a novel lived in my head. He was determined to break it from its prison. He hugged me through his eyes.

My mother's crying on the front porch. I'm stopped in front of our house, still tripping on acid; rain falls in jagged lines on the window. A chasm grows between my parents and I. What could you expect of someone born with such a large head and a small hole in their heart? Would they not think of the worst ways to fill it?

When I was young, they praised my appetite. It was a good sign for a child to eat. Sweet meats and sour candies. I liked best fried chicken and Coca-Cola.

My dad was happy to feed me. Fried chicken in his childhood was climbing a tree to steal robin eggs. He heard of carbonated sugar beverages on the radio. He heard Bob Dylan sing "Blowin' In The Wind." He dreamed in a language he didn't yet speak.

Years later, infatuated with a counterculture that died at the Altamont Free Festival while my mother was being born, I would listen to Dylan. His electric cries streamed from the cloud, straight to the speakers of our family's Ford. My dad winced, the gentle melody he'd heard crackling through his radio all those years and miles ago seemed distorted beyond comprehension.

I followed the gentle rounding curves of I-84. Tracing the edges of the Columbia River westward. I remember driving across the ridges of America's spine. Filling North Dakota's prairie potholes with theories of glacial movement. Fighting through the narrow curves of Lookout Pass, and emerging on the other side of the Rockies.

My parents traveled west to fill their bellies. I went west to go to college. I'd study something practical, like marketing.

Art didn't say anything. He must have lamented my decision, but he was too wise to argue or to judge. He just told me how it was, what would happen next for him. Art knew who I was. But maybe he too couldn't perceive my lowest frequencies. He was white. His parents didn't give up their language, customs, and family to raise him. What debts did he owe? Certainly none to a tiger mom.

I FaceTimed him from my campus reflecting pool. Mt. Hood loomed large over a clear blue day.

I can't play Jazz anymore. I don't know, something happened. I hurt my hand. I had a falling out. I just can't do it, it doesn't work. Art would be fine. He wanted to make electronic music. He was going to be a DJ. Following the prophets of the 90s who broadcasted their gospel of electric hip-hop and techno through pirate radio stations.

I wrote a research paper that won an award. I called Art on his birthday. He sounded tired. His firecracker curls depressed and tied back in a bun. There wasn't much light in his eye. I didn't tell him about the paper.

I was in the library when my mother called. I was writing a thesis when she told me the police found Art on the banks of the Mississippi. I grabbed at my pen, sucked in through my teeth.

I didn't cry. That was just like Art: 12 bars, cut short. A blue note stuck sour between olive thumbs and string.

I didn't make it to the funeral. I finished my thesis on Charley Patton. Art would have liked that. I did it because I knew what a semester of school cost. He wouldn't have cared for that.

Years later, I wrote taglines that sold shoes. I wrote calls to action and campaign messages that seduced the subconscious. Amelia and I drove out of Portland to find forest. She came from California. I didn't know that they had suburbs as banal as mine. But they must have, for she marveled at the trees like I did.

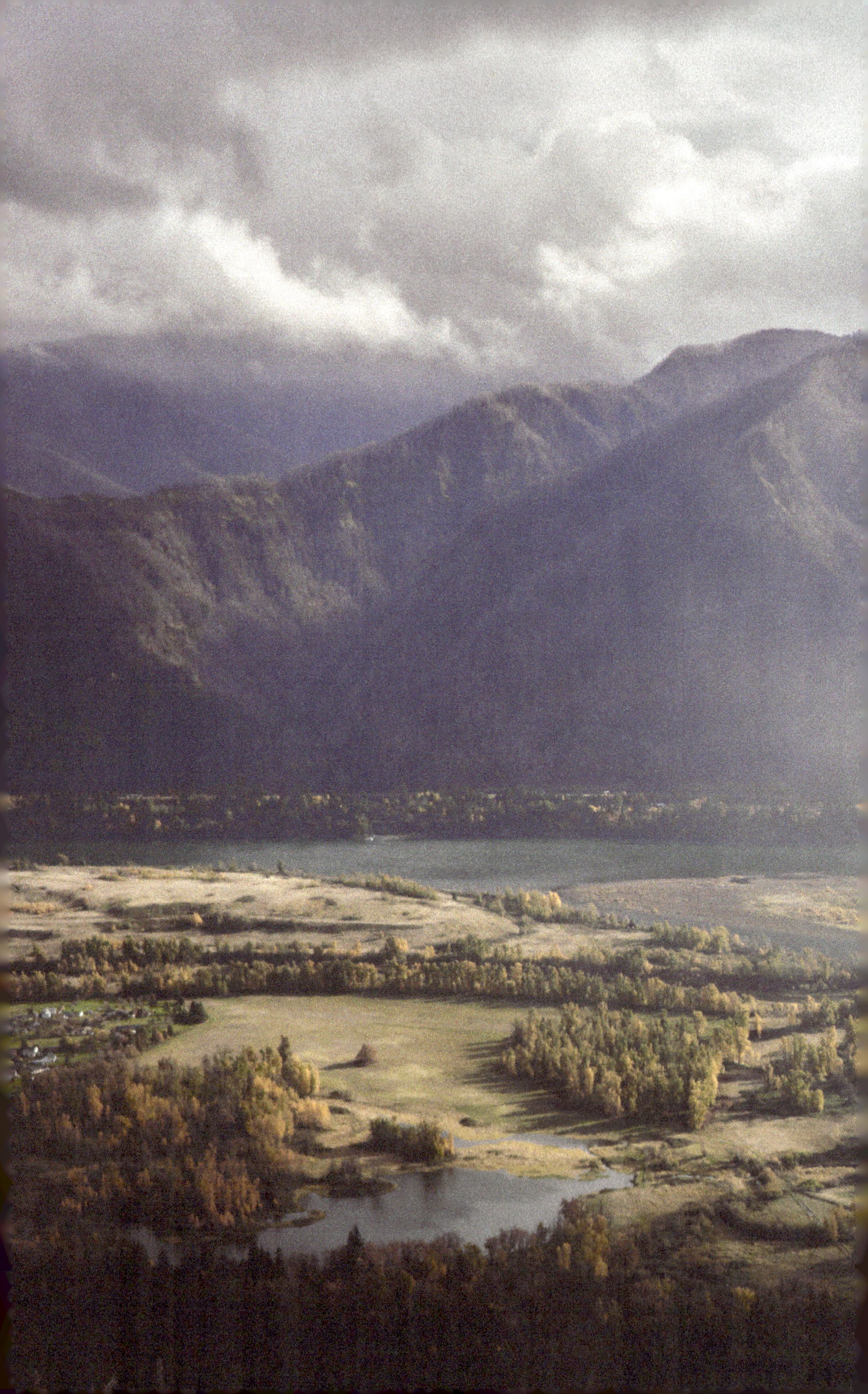

A gorge is
the ghost of
a mountain
turned
upside down,
pinched on
either side by
plateaus that
won't mend.
They join
together at
the bottom.

Didn't you have the redwoods?

California is bigger and emptier than you think.

I told Amelia that The Twin Cities were full of life and teeming with culture. Don't be fooled by the lack of coastline and evergreens. There was a vibrant jazz scene. Have you even heard of Fat Kid Wednesdays? Did you know David King played with Dewey Redmon, Jeff Beck, Bill Frisell, and Art Warren?

We hiked under pine, hearing but not seeing the river that ran alongside. The land seemed interrupted. A long line of desire drawn in its very heart, flowing west to the ocean: a septum running between two high ridges.

A healthy heart has a septum, a wall that separates left and right ventricles. My septum had a hole.

The America I knew was covered in cornfields. I didn't mind. I liked the way they blanketed the earth. They reminded me of China. My father took me once to the village he grew up in. His father was buried there; a ridge of plateau steppes overlooking farmland ancient with golden dust.

I drive out in the morning. Amelia wants to sleep in, but I go to greet Sunrise in the valley. I see the Columbia wide and lilting, the rising sun dancing in stanzas along the ripple of water-lines.

I press a button to switch from Amelia's language app bleating Chinese phrases and translations. She was learning; to impress my relatives when we visit. Springsteen is on the radio. His synthesizer playing sparse enough for each downbeat of the snare to punctuate the small space left by the last note. I could never hear clearly what he said in his verses, but I know how it felt. I hear him loud and clear in the refrain.

Static sounds in my ear. The road ahead overgrows with roots that gnarl across the black pavement. I rub my eyes, trying to blink the image away. The roots linger, but my eyes sting with soapy teardrops. My car bounces over the roots and gets caught. I leave it behind, Springsteen shouts after me in Mandarin.

Gorge in Chinese is written 峽 (Xiá). Its photo-etymology translates roughly to mountain (山) pinched between (夾). And phonetically, sounds alluringly close to the word for descent.

I'm descending now, past the end of the road, the wailing of a tube amp eating its own feedback in my ear. Over the edge of the cliff and down, down into the water, where the noise is muffled.

A gorge is the ghost of a mountain turned upside down, pinched on either side by plateaus that won't mend. They join together at the bottom.


I'm going down into the water to find that bottom. I kick my legs, ripping backwards prayer hands past my ribs. My lungs fill with blood and my heart pumps air.

In the depths, between two rising ridges, I find a pocket. A cavern just big enough for a body. The hole in my septum, a space just big enough for an olive pit.

There, underneath the water, I hear the music that slips in between the notes. The protolanguage rings clear. Plato speaks in aphorisms, leaves Bai Di early in the morning. Li Bai writes in Free Indirect Discourse. I see visions of the ancestors pinned to a cross. Art plays nocturnes on a dulcimer strung with pearls. His hair dancing red and green in the water. Winks at me as the current pulls me by.

By.

I pull myself out onto the bank on the other side of the Columbia. I'm dressed in black at the back of a funeral. I walk towards the side of a cliff, passing gray and graying crosses, finding my father. He turns to face me, unclasps his hands, and reaches to shake mine.

A sleek mahogany casket stands next to a hollow plot.

> We are gathered here today to celebrate the life of Wang Wen Xia, a dutiful father and husband; beloved by many.

I hear horns and drums in the hills. It distracts me from the rites. My father leans over: don't worry about that, it's not for us.

In the depths, between two rising ridges, I find a pocket. A cavern just big enough for a body.

Looking up, past the headstone to a pathway carved in the gorge's side, I see another funeral. A martial bugle cries in a tin falsetto, drums strum along a pentatonic procession. They carry the son of the deceased in their arms. Up above, I see this lively line of people walking a thin trail between the trees. They're wearing white and chasing the setting sun. I'm seven years old; I ask my dad what they are doing.

They're marching to dispel evil spirits. Tradition dictates a son to cry and fight his way back towards the casket. It's the job of the funeral procession to keep him from getting there.

> Ashes to ashes
> Dust to dust

The casket drops indelibly into the hole. The river runs out to the ocean. This is as far as you can go before west turns back to face the east.

119

# HA

# COLU

Poetry by Maxwell Kline

IL

MBIA!

anything for comfort and
""HAIL COLUMBIA!"" ravenous,
vegan diesel cold rubber brake-
violence (ONE LOOK ONE LOOK) empty
sheets/slops of rain slapping
white streaks nail polish as divination
vas deferens topped off with
WILL BE GREEN AND FINE))) intentional
metal try!again!try!again later
cold "OLYMPIA BEER It's the Water" and
flesh intestines light gray in the
in your mouth it's safe just ask Columbus from
from PVC: milk,tube,exposure to
liquid (FROM THE STARS) and black
the aisle hands moving quickly
try to speak but milk dribbles
your leaking herringbone collar
lips ((((WESTERN MAN YOU'VE MISSED
fawns leap down your levistraus&co517s ((BOOTCUT)) their hoof prints
concrete announcers who don't know the senate is again
milk~stained~kindergarten~blue
FACE LOOKING WEST)) but bound
soul!lucky!soul!lucky!soul your
life into recycled,PET,seat-covers,,,

a theorized death by PVC: c r e e p , c r a v e , c r a w l , t o w a r d s pad fear.of.plastic/on/plastic black!plastic!ashtray but for the ever-loving windshield check for organs spread on the dashboard microplastics says: (((YOUR CHILDREN design w/ so much lip smacking fingertipsblackandailingalwaysso ""HAIL COLUMBIA""" soft pink salmon dying light cud for a stranger's spit across the train a theorized death sunlightpolyvinylchlorideakalove hole trains!trains!trains across and sharp opening your stomach only red killer whale tears over leaking!leaking over dry cracked YOURSTOP))))) segments of your steaming (BIG ONE) silver bile will leave stains no atrium no families alone under talking about daylight savings watch: you're a part of (ONE LINE) crypt carpet seats your ((EMPTYING for ((COLUMBIA CITY)) what a lucky immaculate corpse breathes new demands action !!! """"HAIL COLUMBIA!"""""

# BLEAK THRILLS

Excerpt from a comic by Ree Artemisa

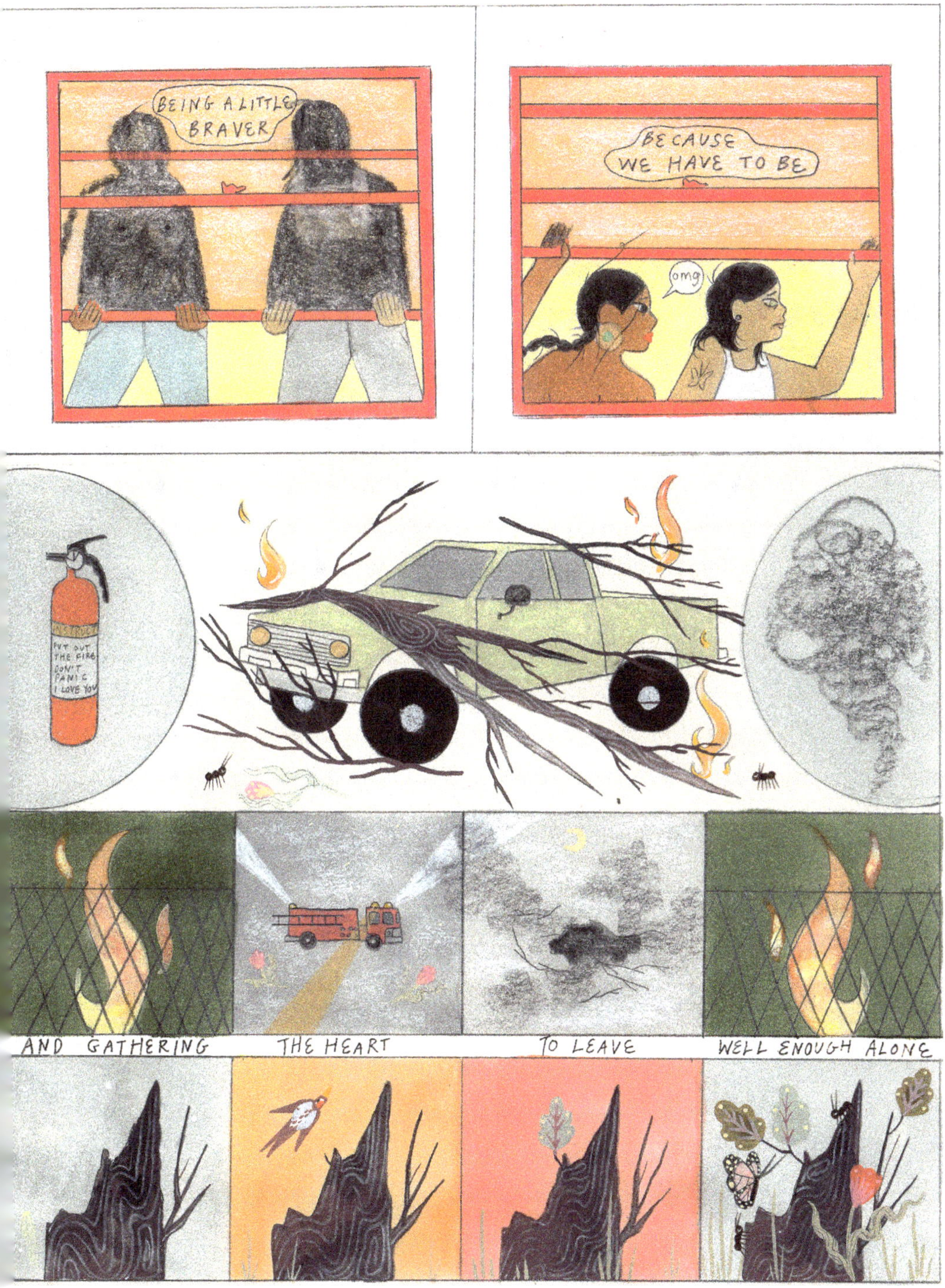

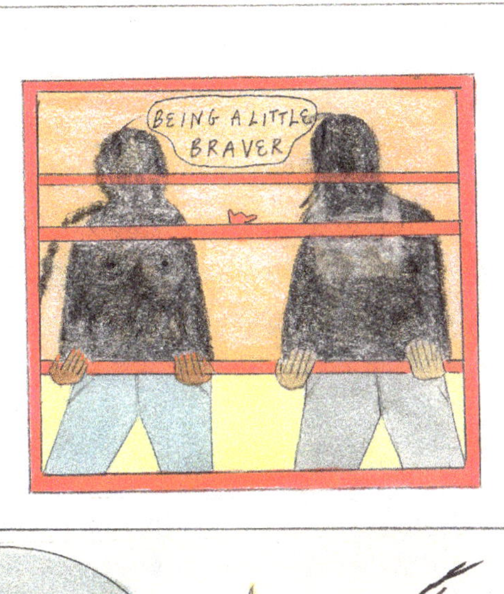


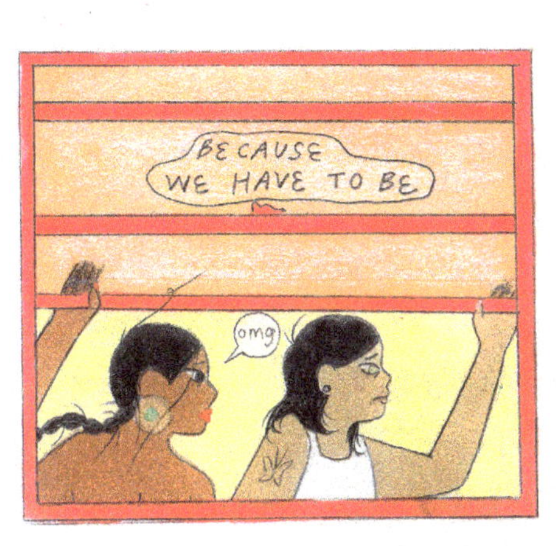




AND GATHERING    THE HEART    TO LEAVE    WELL ENOUGH ALONE

# FRAC PAN

Creative Non-Fiction by Alicia Johnson

TURED

GEA

Collage by Stephanie Hatch

The landscape reveals itself in flashes of headlight and shadow. Interstate 84 makes its way through the corner of Eastern Oregon where I was born, a valley tucked between the Blue Mountains and the Eagle Cap Wilderness, the road twisting down to sea level to follow the Columbia River as it slips ceaseless toward the Pacific Ocean. In the daylight, there are wind farms with giant blades turning white and jagged in fields and cliffs overlooking the water. Windsurfers harness the same celestial breezes that funnel through the gorge on a personal scale, leaping over whitecaps, sprinkling the river like vibrating confetti. As the road winds further along, temperate rainforests emerge, elegant waterfalls cascade down higher cliffs as silver kinetic threads among the velvet greenery.

We lost the daylight behind the blunt edge of the mountain range somewhere in the Blues, a desolate stretch of ponderosa pine-forested highway with side roads named things like, "poverty flats" and dotted with places for trucks to pull off in desperation if their brakes fail. We approach the river in darkness, that wet physical barrier between the homeland of my childhood and my husband LeGrand's, but instead of windmills and waterfalls I found a trail of red taillights eyeing me in the blackness, the cool September air thick and swift and full of dread.

There is a glow inside the van as my husband drives. My three-year-old son, Timothy, sits chubby-legged in his five-point-harness car seat, peeking through sleepy, dark eyelashes at whatever Disney film we put in the van entertainment system to endure this ninety-minute stretch of the drive. So much of parenting early childhood is modular: naptimes and playtimes and storytimes and craft times and bath times and mealtimes and screentime. Travel upsets almost all of this, and my morning-sick, pregnant mantra is simply: *get through.* Frederick, my five-year-old bobs his head gently in sleep on a hungry-hungry-caterpillar neck pillow. Wesley, my firstborn, my dinosaur-loving, *Lord of the Rings*-obsessed seven-year-old is gasping for air.

I listen to him wheeze, counting his rattling breaths, waiting for the cough: the barking exhalations wearing out his little body. We've mapped out the hours, the minutes between inhaler treatments. We were given prednisone tablets the night before that he refuses to choke down, no matter the sugar content of the food in which we try to disguise it. So LeGrand speeds, pushing the van faster through the dark corridors of rock where the water has worn the earth down over centuries, a primeval trail of water molecules rushing instinctively to the pull of the ocean. I pray, rubbing my swollen belly where two babies float, a pair of split-cell, win-the-lottery-odds miracles oblivious to anything but the drum of my heartbeat, the vague peripheries of my voice, the unexpected rumble of my intestines.

My body registers the internal combustion of pregnancy incredibly early—millions of invisible telegraph wires firing wildly between the pituitary to the follicle to the forming placenta, my bloodstream awash in the dots and dashes of secret communique. The silent agents of hormone subterfuge cause my body to rebel, to reject food and drink for the nine months of gestating interloper. Nausea is my earliest indicator. Summer

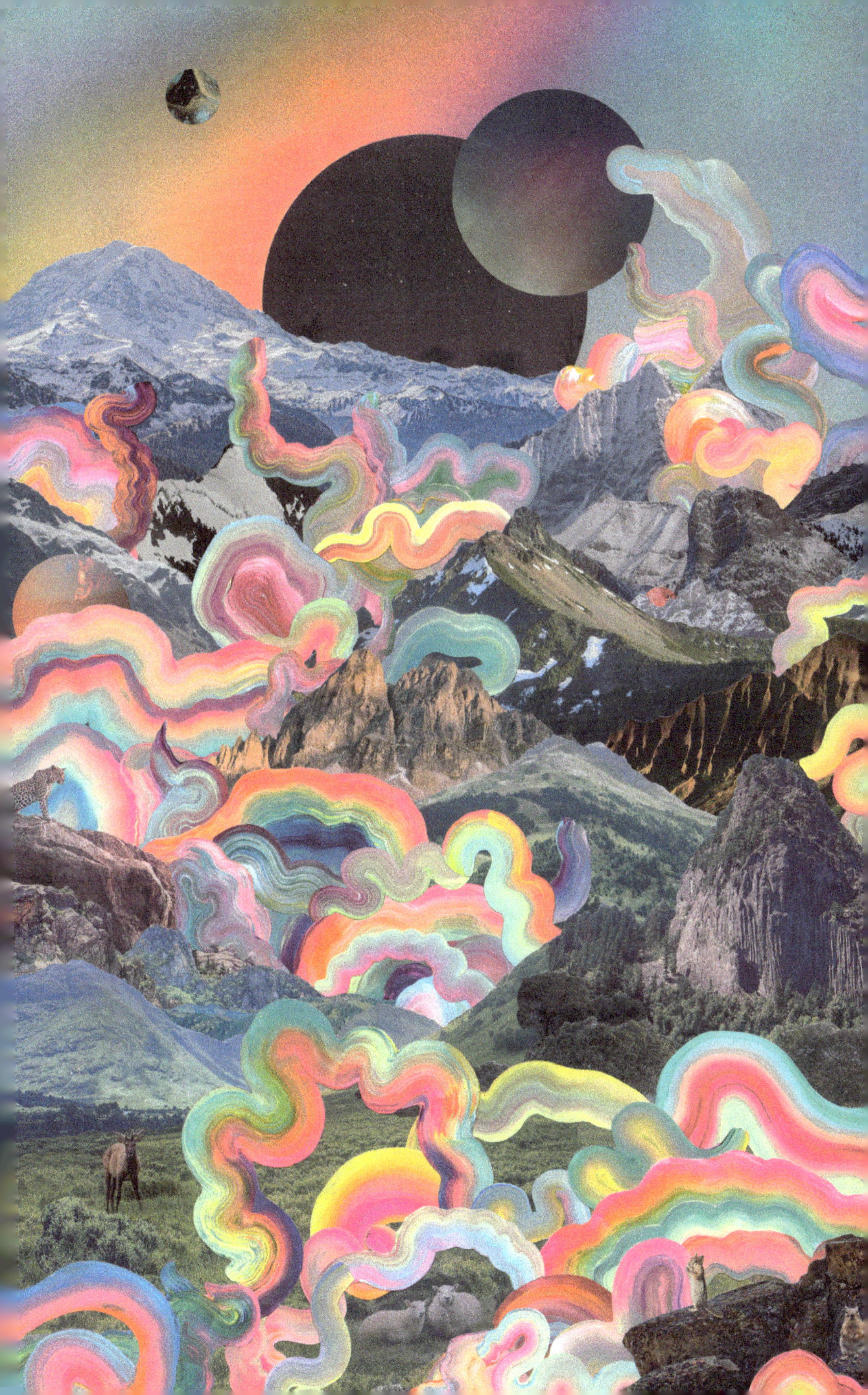

was at its peak when I started throwing up. By early August I was already getting IV fluids from the emergency department, pediatric phlebotomists searching for my collapsed veins with tiny butterfly needles.

It's standard practice at my obstetrician's office to schedule a ten-week ultrasound to rule out any problems and confirm the estimated due date. A middle-aged sonographer chatted with me while she began the exam. I'd been through enough pregnancies to read reactions, so when she made a nondescript noise, followed by a pause, warning bells began to clang inside my heart as I sank from the high delight of hearing the heartbeat swoosh on the monitor. My thoughts shuffled through all the possible scenarios of things that could go wrong—I'd taken enough biology classes to understand the quagmire of meiosis, the replicating cells, the genome splicing and reconfiguring, the hormone-triggering dance that was so impossibly complex. I knew missteps were frequent and many.

**Our instincts sharpen, our dreams grow more vivid, atavistic.**

She laughed—an experienced, deep chuckle. "Do you see it?"

My mouth must have been agape, staring at the grainy screen, not gleaning any recognizable information from the shifting inkblot outline, on what may as well have been a Rorschach test for parenthood.

"There's two. You're having twins."

I heard myself involuntarily repeating a mantra of disbelief: *Oh my gosh, oh my gosh, oh my gosh.* I'd become a looping .gif, the incredulous twin mom, my brain not accepting the new reality inside of my body. I had never wanted twins—the logistics of one of me outnumbered by the unrelenting, seemingly unfillable depths of newborn needs.

She took lots of images, explaining that they were identical and she couldn't see a membrane separating them, so I would be referred to a specialist who had more advanced equipment and could tell for certain.

Three weeks later I found myself at the research hospital in Portland, in a sleek room with a blonde, white lab coat-wearing sonographer taking painstaking images and measurements. The appointment was booked for an hour, so I settled myself onto the exam table and relaxed, enjoying the safety of watching the twins as she worked. Pregnancy is mostly a blind endeavor. We try to read the tea leaves, discern symptoms and twinges, and rely on old wives' tales for prehistoric wisdom passed down through generations. Our instincts sharpen, our dreams grow more vivid, atavistic.

Following the ultrasound, I was ushered into an adjoining office, crammed between an older perinatologist and a younger doctor who carried a notebook and said little. The older doctor spent no time feeding me soft words or innocuous small talk. He got down to the cruelly impartial mathematics of my situation. This kind of twins, monoamniotic-monochorionic, was extremely rare and carried with them an extensive list of complications. Best case scenario saw me inpatient in the hospital for continuous observation at 28 weeks, to deliver by planned cesarean at 32 weeks, followed by a mandatory NICU stay. Among a long list of less desirable outcomes was a condition called twin-to-twin transfusion syndrome (TTTS), in which case I would be helicoptered to Seattle or San Francisco for emergency surgery. Worst case scenario, their delicate amniotic chords became entangled, and they would both die from lack of oxygen.

He bluntly asked me if I was seeing a therapist. When I said no, he ordered me to get one. "You'll need it," he said. "Those babies can die at any moment."

LeGrand's beloved grandmother passed away in late September. She'd lived a quiet but meaningful life, making everyone lucky enough to know her feel seen and unconditionally loved. An unassuming woman who lived her life on a farm, she baked decadent cinnamon rolls that she lavished on her friends and family. Not wanting to miss the opportunity to pay our final respects, we loaded the kids in the van and headed east.

One of the many members of the extended family visited our hotel room while we were getting ready for the funeral service. She was full of good-news energy, telling LeGrand how she was acquainted with a pediatrician, so naturally, she consulted him about my condition.

"He told me that you don't have to worry because medical technology has improved so much over the past few years, so it's not as big of a deal to have babies prematurely."

I felt a combination of hurt and anger rise among the ocean of anxiety where I was already capsizing, taking on more and more water every day. She couldn't understand that I wasn't worried about the NICU stay—I was worried about getting them there.

When I expressed the rationale for my fears, I was again dismissed with a line about how if God took them, He must need them more than we did.

I didn't believe in that kind of God.

Our room in the OHSU pediatric emergency department was not created for comfortable overnight stays. There was a small mounted television on the wall across from the hospital bed with a pre-loaded selection of children's programming. Wesley's tastes tended toward dinosaur documentaries, mixed with a little *Star Wars*, as he began to outgrow the Lightning McQueen phase that defined his toddler years. Hospital beds are not cozy or particularly soft, resulting in a restless shifting of limbs under thin blankets, finger caught in the red-light kiss of a pulse oximeter, face partially obscured by an oxygen mask.

I remember staring with relentless intensity at the monitor measuring his heartbeat and blood oxygen saturation. After a series of nebulizer treatments, he was hovering around 88%. We couldn't be discharged until he was at least 94%. The pharmacy on campus concocted an oral version of prednisone mixed in some kind of syrup I could only imagine was part witchery since it was successfully ingested, and now we waited for the steroid to ease the inflammation in his airway, to release its hold on the tight labyrinth of tubes filling with mucus.

My phone sat charging on the floor, part entertainment device (Wesley liked a game where monkeys popped balloons), part lifeline back to my little apartment in Lake Oswego where my husband was trying, unsuccessfully, to grab a few hours of sleep before heading to his accounting job across the river that bisects the city. The hospital sits on the west hills of Portland, a region locals affectionately call, "pill hill" because of the several hospitals, including this sprawling research and teaching campus. Slowly, dawn began lifting the chill, heavy fingers of darkness outside the window behind my chair, signaling the end of what felt like an interminable journey across two states to this anxious vigil. I knew with the brightening horizon my mom would be traveling the I-5 corridor from Salem to Portland, past sleeping tulip and iris fields, blue herons pausing, frozen like scarecrows among furrowed soil before

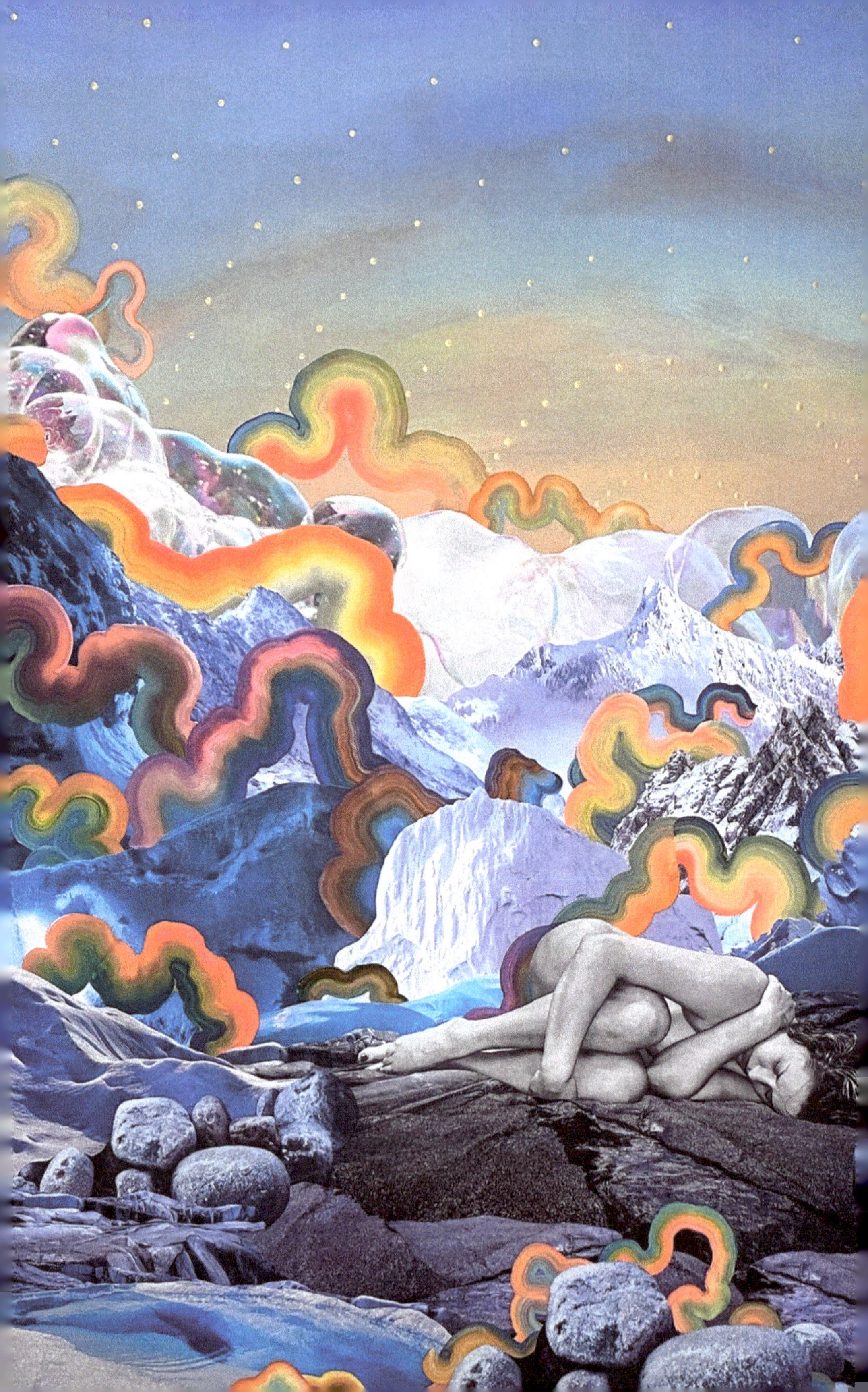

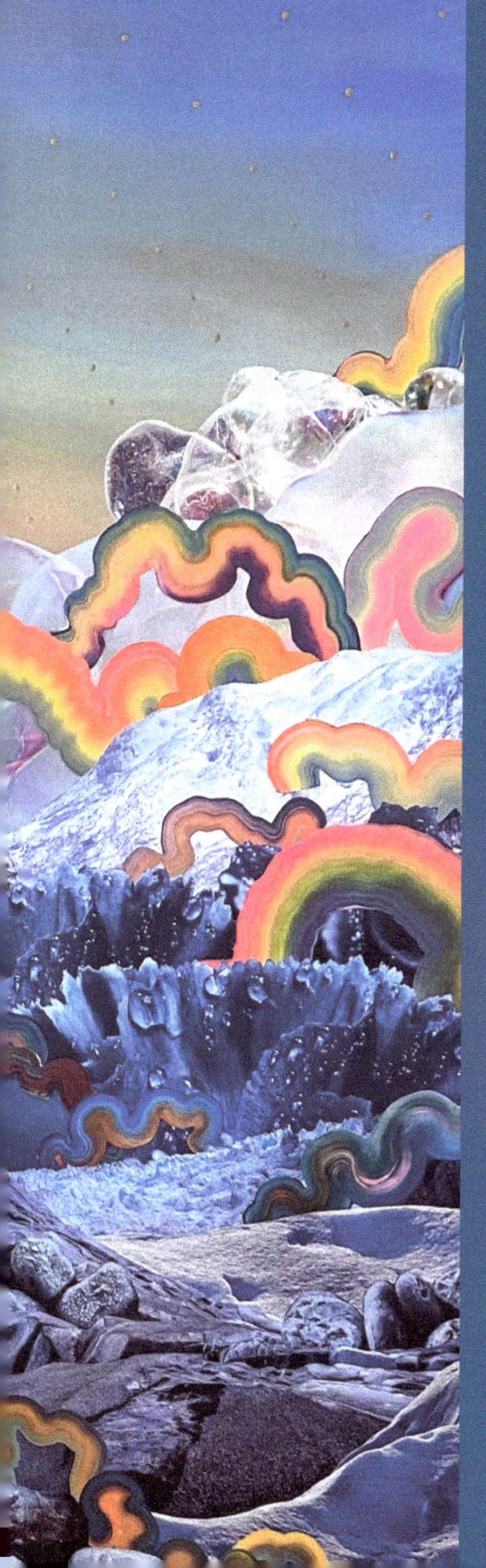

Slowly, dawn began lifting the chill, heavy fingers of darkness outside the window behind my chair, signaling the end of what felt like an interminable journey across two states to this anxious vigil.

the early mists evaporated in the stronger sunlight.

LeGrand calls to tell me that one of the tires on his car is flat: he's taking it to the garage to be repaired while he works. My mom helps my middle son board the kindergarten bus, lunch in backpack, a ritual kiss on the swirl of his hair, then drives LeGrand to meet us at the hospital. This unexpected hiccup in our already difficult morning lends a secondary brightness to my day, a little consolation prize tucked into the mixed bag from the universe: it will allow LeGrand and Wesley to attend a perinatology ultrasound appointment I have scheduled across the hospital campus in a few hours.

The room where they performed the ultrasound was cool with low, theatrically dimmed lights that allowed the flatscreen where the invisible vibrations from the wand transmitted to glow with greater brilliance. I lay back on the table, happy, exhausted, and relaxed. Given five minutes of quiet, I would have fallen asleep.

The technician tucked a towel into the front of my leggings to protect my clothes from the jelly—a strange contradiction of feeling simultaneously warm and cold on my exposed abdomen. There would have been small talk, the white noise surrounding the real reason we were there: to check on the twins.

The wand came down on my belly and all I could see was profound, shattering stillness. There was no rush of blood, no pulsing, no whoosh of heartbeat. It came with a certainty that cut to the core, a seismic rupture in my soul that needed no confirmation from the suddenly flustered technician who began muttering awkwardly about needing to check things, take measurements. I remember my heart sending out a brief flare of hope that maybe the other one had survived until she moved the wand and I saw both babies, floating side by side in the darkness, so incomprehensibly, hopelessly perfect. I couldn't tear my eyes away from that high-resolution screen. Why had nature created such exquisite roundness, little snub noses, tiny fists brought cuddle-close. It was such an evolutionary waste.

I was given a box of tissues and led into a room where I sat alone. I don't know where Wesley and LeGrand were taken. My soul swirled inward around a new dark center of gravity. I waited for a doctor to come and explain the obvious, the ineffectual platitudes, the next steps. Somewhere down the hall I heard sobbing, and wondered if the nurse had broken down as well.

They gave me three options, choose your own adventure: trauma edition. I could let nature take its course, eventually going into labor at home when my body finally registered the loss. I could take a pill to speed things along. Or I could visit the abortion clinic on campus, open every Friday by appointment. I couldn't bear the thought of walking around like a human sepulcher, and I couldn't imagine going through it at home without the help of drugs. I didn't want to be awake for this. I gratefully chose door number three.

They shepherded me out a back entrance, so I wouldn't have to see the still-expectant mothers in the waiting room, their still unshattered lives intact. Getting home was a blur—I remember giving my husband my phone and telling him to handle any talking with people. It hurt too much to communicate with anyone. I clung to him and blocked out the rest of the world. Each breath was a struggle, a negotiation to go on.

I lay in bed, trying to sleep, hoping for some relief in oblivion. My three-year-old, a quirky cherub with a profound speech delay, climbed up on my bed, turned *Curious George* on the television, and sat quietly patting my leg with his dimpled hand.

Driving to the hospital in the early autumn light, the leaves were a wash of impressionist color to my unfocused, tear-dry eyes. I was numb to their vibrancy, to the dull reflection of the river playing hide-and-seek to our right, the friendly canopy of trees. The local classical music station announced the passing of Sir Neville Marriner, the longtime conductor of the Academy of Saint Martin in the Fields. His music had become the soundtrack to the highs and lows of my life. I had fallen in love with my husband to Neville Marriner conducting Ralph Vaughan William's haunting *Fantasia on a Theme* by Thomas Tallis. Now, as his melodies carried me ever closer to my destination, the moment of final separation, he was conducting a ghostly, posthumous dirge.

I would be coming home from the hospital this time with no new baby in my arms. There was no car seat carefully installed, no ball bearing floating in a ring indicating if the seat was perfectly parallel to the road. No diaper bag packed with a curated tiny outfit to come home in, no miniature diapers and onesies and burp clothes or binkies tucked in pockets. Instead, in a few weeks, I would get a call from a funeral home where I could pick up a plain white box of ashes.

The placenta, the organ that grows in the womb to sustain new life, grows webs of blood vessels like branches of a tree. Stretching down like the deepest root is the cord that channels the nourishment and oxygen to the growing fetus. Sloughed-off cells catch a ride through the tree of life into the garden of its mother bloodstream, there to linger for months, even years.

Those broken-off pieces from the tiny continent grow and shapeshift along preconfigured tectonic plates, migrating invisibly. Grieving follows no textbook-delineated rules. You find yourself wandering in a world disrupted, chasing mirages. I couldn't sleep, couldn't turn off my brain, couldn't run away from the tripwires of this new world.

I remember laying on my bed, facing the bathroom, staring into the vast nothing of my own woundedness. The hurt felt so overwhelming, I would have done anything to make it stop. Anything. If I left, I would feel nothing, find relief, finally rest. If I stayed, I had three sons and a husband who needed me. I felt myself floating inexorably toward the precipice. I had to make a choice.

If I left, I knew there would be extended family there to help pick up the pieces, but my boys would never be the same. LeGrand would never be the same.

If I stayed, we would attend every harvest festival the greater Portland area had to offer. We would eat roasted corn and drink cider slushies at Bauman Farms. We would go to Sauvie Island for a corn maze and doughnuts. We would travel to EZ orchards where Timmy would stuff his face with pumpkin spice doughnuts and ride the horses and hayrides. We would ride the Polar Express in Hood River, and almost get stranded in a winter storm. We would write letters to Santa and paint ugly Christmas sweaters and watch Will Ferrell dressed in an elf costume and remember how to laugh.

And we did.

I would choose to try for one more baby, I would walk into another ultrasound room, knowing that I would remember everything that happened before in full-scale, technicolor detail.

I would open my eyes when the wand met my stomach, pressing down hard and cold and impersonal. The screen would light up with fuzzy outlines as the technician searched for landmarks within my internal wilderness. When the image came into focus, there would be two clear outlines, two tiny universes side by side in the celestial substrate. Spontaneous twins. Again.

# LAST RIDE

# RIDE

# GREAT

Fiction by Rich Perin

# OF THE DIVIDE

I was flush with cash and dropping three grand for a 1981 Cadillac Coupe Deville seemed like a reasonable extravagance. The previous owner was a retired state trooper from a small town 70 miles outside Portland. The car was his pride and joy, a royal ride to revel in for his sunset years. The old trooper spent extra reconditioning and customizing it, painting the exterior Spanish blue with white pinstripes, coated-spoked hubcaps, cushioned Landau roof, inside reupholstered with leather. He didn't add too many miles, though—taking the Caddy out only on Sundays to church then Dairy Queen afterwards, sharing a banana split with his wife. Routine like that for several years then diabetes got to him, and he lost a leg to it, which ended his will to drive, so he sold the cruiser with some regret, hoping the next owner would treat it right for future generations to enjoy.

The Caddy was a fiend for fuel and drank as if drinking for three, but shamingly the thirst didn't translate into speed or power. Maintaining anything above 65 was a struggle.

But it was the smoothest ride I've ever wheeled. Driving from the comfort of a couch. Featherlight steering, floating on air, the car didn't handle like a massive stretch of steel, pistons, and chrome. It was more like a deep-shag magic carpet ride.

The Caddy was the first time I got the car I wanted instead of the car I could afford. The choice was liberating, not the practical approach, but a far more interesting one, a reinvigoration that reminded me of forks in the road of life: same-old same-old or something else. Wanting to affirm the reclaimed spirit of adventure, as well as build a bond with the Caddy, the very next day the coupe and I set out on a road trip, to somewhere we both had never been.

Oregon's wilderness is broad spectrum. Its coast is moody and cragged, cut from stormy seas. Inland from the Pacific, pines, ferns, and moss layer then climb the appropriately named Cascade Mountains, where raindrops accumulate, stream down to waterfalls, into crystal clear wild-salmon tributaries. The eastern side of the Cascades is starkly different, suffers a rain shadow, any clouds that manage to climb over the mountains are spent. The evergreenery fizzles out, cannot sustain, vegetation and landscape progresses to barren, then turns moonscape in Oregon's southeast corner, where people are fewer and further in between.

The Caddy and I headed to that remote corner, the Alvord Desert, which is a dry lakebed for most of the year. Eighty square miles of flat nothing, no need for a road, as you can drive in any direction without worry of obstacles, a collide-less expanse, enough room where world land speed records are attempted and sometimes fall. Even though I knew the Caddy wouldn't muster much speed, I liked the idea of letting it roll in an open space, where the brake pedal is forgettable.

In late autumn, the crisp higher altitudes of the Steens Mountains slunk down the slopes, a dry chill, but the sun sharp, the sky glared, the climes ideal for a leisurely drive, windows down.

Under the wheels was akin to fine gravel, I could hear the grind, I knew that if I floored the pedal the big rear-wheeled drive would spin ungripped, kick up dirt and make a rusty dust storm, so I set the pace steady with no sudden change in direction. I evaluated the steering, the Caddy pulled a little left but with a tap from time to time, a nudge to the right, a straight line was mostly achieved. About 10 minutes into the Alvord, I let the Caddy take the lead, releasing the grip from the steering wheel to unscrew a thermos of coffee, poured myself a mug, and smeared a bagel. Automatic driving with no computer AI at the helm, or camera eyes or sensors, just the car's soul, and I looked to the Steens, thinking how they grabbed the moisture up high in the atmosphere, stacked its peaks with snow and ice, ridiculous features in contrast to rain-shadowed, barren flats of Alvord lakebed that can't hold a puddle.

I wasn't driving fast, the cruise control at 35, but after eating the bagel and daydreaming, I lost sense of direction. I was looking to the horizons, trying to identify which mountain was what, when a quarter mile ahead I saw an enormous parked red pickup with a flapping American flag. Next to it was a red, white, and blue canopy tent. Hooked to the back of the truck was a custom barbecue trailer, holding a long 60-gallon barrel smoker. Its chimney was puffing, and a small, old man with a chef's hat stood over it. He was wearing a red polo shirt tucked into his jeans. His smile beamed, and he waved a marinade brush at me. I pulled over and lowered the window. "Hi there," I said. "That smoker is impressive."

The man chuckled. "Kind of you to notice. I'm trying to barbecue in all fifty states, so I need a quality rig that lasts."

"Looks bulletproof."

"Ha! Maybe so!" He held out his hand, his smile never slipped, sustaining its intensity and degree. "My name is Jett Chisum, I'm from Wyoming."

I returned a firm shake, looked straight into his eyes, and matched his grin. "Pleased to meet you, Jett. My name is Rich. I'm from Portland."

"Portland? You don't say? Out here is a little different than Portland, huh?"

"Sure is, Jett. It's nice to get out in the open, see a different view, take a double lung-full of breath. Inflates the soul."

"Sure does, Rich. You got a nice way of saying it. I hear an accent, too. You from New Zealand?"

I shook my head and told him where I was born and raised. "But I've been in the States since I was 18."

"Well, your timing is good, Rich," said Jett. "I'm just finishing up cooking, letting the meat rest in cold smoke for 40 minutes or so before it's ready for eating. Been at it since four this morning. You're most welcome to share a meal with me. I got more than plenty."

> **The big and quiet puts things in perspective. A good place to recenter oneself.**

I took a closer look at Jett's camp. There were Jesus and political party affiliation stickers on the back of his truck. Arranged on the cab roof were three sets of deer antlers. A gun rack with a rifle hung on the rear window. Jett was bald and I could see that one of his ears wasn't there anymore. He was small and stout, moved stiffly, like he had fallen off a horse a lot and now aged, his well of flexibility was filled with concrete. His face was wrinkled and sun-damaged, but his eyes were an earnest blue. And his smile seemed genuine. I put the Caddy in park and turned off the engine.

"You know, Jett, it's not everyday that barbecue appears in a desert. Free, too.

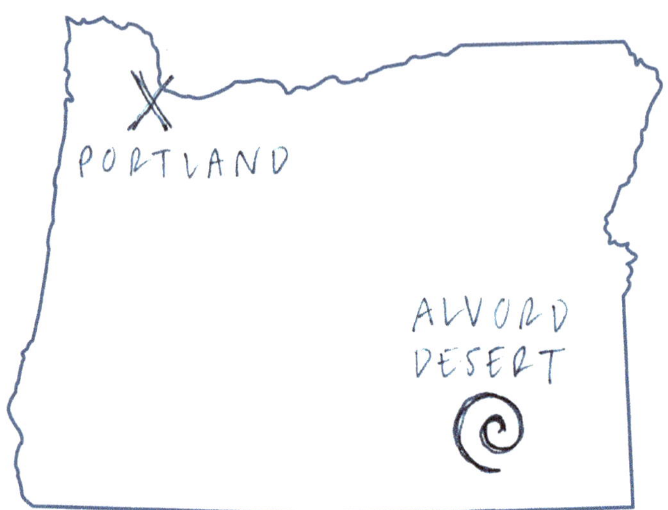


The universe has suggested it so, so yes, thank you. I accept your kind invitation."

As I got out of the Caddy, Jett said, "That sure is a beautiful car, Rich. You don't see too many of them anymore." He walked around it, kicking tires, admired the chrome. "Yep, that's when they still put silverware on the bumpers. Real pretty."

"American steel, old American sculpture, from a long-ago era," I said, and then told him the story of the previous owner.

"I appreciate that, Rich," said Jett. "Good to remember history. It's the way to honor it." Jett pointed to the fold-up table where supplies were set under the tent. "Come on over, I'll get you a drink. You like wine?"

"Wine? Uh, sure."

"I can't drink hard liquor anymore and beer gives me gas, but I come to find out I like wine. Besides, we're having brisket, grass-raised. Red wine, red meat, good eating."

Two outdoor reclining lounge chairs were set up but no one else was around. Jett gestured one for me, and opened a cooler that was positioned between the two chairs. "Half-bottles, Rich. The best way to enjoy," he said while uncorking a half-bottle, then passing it over to me. "This is a fizzy Italian red. Served chilled. I got other kinds if you want something else."

I waited for a glass, but Jett uncorked another for himself, settled, and resigned into his lounge chair facing North to the Steens, which he set his eyes to as he sipped straight from the half-bottle. I leaned back likewise.

"So why in hell's name you decided to come out here, Rich?"

"A road trip with my new car seemed in order, Jett. I've never been out this way. And I am averse to crowds, this seems like the most crowdless place in the state. I imagine the Coupe Deville enjoys total roadless unconstraint, too."

"Oh, yeah, I guess it's a good place to drive that car. It is a land yacht, for sure, and this here is land yacht heaven."

I pulled a draw from the bottle. The wine was Lambrusco, and it suited the terrain I was in, a refreshing snap with bubbles of possibilities. "And you, Jett, why you out here?"

"I need wide, open spaces where I can barbecue. There are places like this, well, not exactly like this, but unspoiled and uncluttered and quiet. These magical spots are always isolated, always outside of cities. I can't stand cities. I need the sky, Rich, the untouched sky. You ever been to Wyoming, like really back in there, way-out Wyoming, not the Tetons and Yellowstone but the south of the state? That's even a higher desert, feels like no one exists out there but spirits. This here is a high desert, too, but in Wyoming it feels higher. It's a special relationship with the sky."

"Oh yeah, the sky is in your face," I replied. "You get to peer real deep into the universe. The big and quiet puts things in perspective. A good place to recenter oneself."

Jett nodded, then took a sip from his wine bottle. "I bet there are places like this in your home country. You ever want to go home?" he asked. "Seems like this country is hell in a handbasket, and things are gonna get worse."

"Here is my home," I said. "I like it here. I know there are problems, but there are problems everywhere. The US has so much happening. Good things. Bad things. All moving in the fast lane. I don't know if there's another country so diverse. Rio Grande Valley in Texas is different from Bellingham, Washington. Not just different weather or trees or birds, but the people, the food, the culture. I love that. A citizen of this country can travel within its borders and feel like a foreigner. That's righteous."

"Oh, yeah, for sure, Rich, but I feel like a foreigner if I'm in anything bigger than Cheyenne," said Jett, making himself chuckle. "Don't mind dipping my toe into the big smoke from time to time, go to a fancy restaurant, order fancy wine, but I get unsettled in the city if I'm in it for too long."

"I haven't spent much time in Wyoming. A day or two. Where are you from? Cheyenne?"

"Ha! Cheyenne! That's the big smoke! I was born in Cody. In the ghetto."

"Huh? Ghetto in Wyoming?"

"Oh yeah, when I was a kid, dirt poor, it was rough." I noticed that Jett was no longer smiling. "Three-room shotgun house with an outhouse, three brothers and sister, Pa liked his drink, he was heavy on the belt, a spare-the-rod, spoil-the-child man. I got out of there at 14, you tell me that things weren't rough in old Cody, Wyoming. The floors were sawdust, fuses would always blow. You had to light the gas burner an hour before using the hot water."

"Yeah, there are all types of desperations," I said. "You seem to have gone far from those times, though, Jett. This," and I pointed to his truck and trailer, "is not too shabby."

"Oh, for sure, I've done well for myself. I've lifted my family from the dirt, too. You gotta pull people up as you climb. It wasn't easy. I started out as a linesman, stringing wire over the state."

"I assumed you were a rancher."

"Well, I do that some, I just own the land. I was a cowhand for a few years when I was young," said Jett. "My wife is the last lady day-rider in Wyoming. That's how we met."

"A lady day what?"

"Lady day-rider. When you do a round-up you need extra hands to drive the herd, they're called day-riders, and my wife is a lady, and she still gets on a horse and helps out. A lot of folks these days use those all-terrain vehicles, which is a damn shame, it's just lazy and loud. Anyways, she's not my first wife. She's my second. I treat my first wife with respect still, we're friends, we share a son and daughter, but I sure feel lucky I got myself a lady day-rider.

"But electricity," continued Jett, "is what I got big in. I don't know if I'm proud of it."

I didn't ask him why he felt this way and let his comment hang in the air.

The silence prodded more from Jett. "I own the company that strings power lines to mines all over the state. Dakotas, too. Uranium, coal, and now lithium and nickel and rare-earth metals for all the gizmos. I tell you, Rich, they gut the land, dig deep, leave an ugly gash. Makes a hell of a dust, like a cremation." Jett finished the rest of his Lambrusco, then stood up. "I'm going to check the barbecue. Why don't you come look at the Q rig. I made it myself."

It was an impressive barbecue trailer, as long as the Cadillac. Besides the giant smoker barrel, there was another smaller one. The rest of the trailer housed a platform grill, ten-foot square, which could be raised and lowered above a coal bed via a system of chains and gears.

Whatever was cooking smelled intoxicating, a complexity of smoke and sauce and meat. "Man, Jett, this is some set-up," I said.

"I designed and welded it all by myself," responded Jett. He opened the big smoker and a fat brisket, two coiled sausages, and a cloud of sweet smoke appeared. "I soak my chips in wine for a little flair. And I like to use whatevers in the locale. I picked a bunch of knotwood on the way here. I was surprised it burns with a sweet fragrance."

"Portland would love this," I said. "You should set your barbecue rig on a street corner or at a food cart pod. People would line up around the block and drop twenty a plate."

Jett snickered. "I don't know if Portland would take kindly to the likes of me."

"Jett, Portland loves food."

"I can't do any of that vegan stuff. Even my corn bones got belly butter." He opened the smaller smoker, which was on a low heat, revealing a pot of beans, cast iron of cornbread, and rows of husked corn. "The thing is, Rich, there are a lot of angry people these days. Both sides. Left and right. Up and down. Inside out. Everyone's angry, looking for reasons to get angry, waiting to pounce. It's a hell of a way to live. I'm worried I may say or do something wrong and all hell breaking out. I'd rather avoid the trouble altogether."

"Sorry you feel that way," I said. "Portland is more open than you think.

Still, I know what you're talking about. Anger is one way to reach the opposite side, but it doesn't make for much of a bridge."

Jett started preparing platters, one for meat, another for the rest. "These are my special beans," he said spooning some next to the cornbread. "I got hog jowl simmering in it, pearl onions, whole garlic, and of course, mushrooms. Beans absorb the smoke real good, too. Makes me wish we had some duck."

Returning to the chairs, Jett unfolded tv trays and uncorked two half-bottles of merlot. He then insisted we say grace. For some reason I thought he was joking but quickly realized he wasn't. "It's polite to acknowledge the bounty and give thanks to our good fortune," he said.

"Of course." I nodded then bowed my head.

"Lord, we give thanks to the land, the water, and air. Amen." After I affirmed with my amen, Jett stood up. "I almost forgot. We need music." From a wooden box at the back of the tent he returned with a portable record player. He retrieved an album, old country, a scratchy recording of Jimmie Rodgers.

The food was wondrous, with high sweet notes from the sauce that was also heavy on peppercorns, and a peat-like smoke from herbaceous knotwood. The food was soulful, it was evident the process to prepare and cook it was long, and chewing and swallowing unraveled the dedication. It was delicious and I lost attention to what Jett was saying.

"But, yep, that's what I am now," said Jett. "A professional artist. Started five years ago, and I love it. My art sells. I'm represented by a gallery in Pocatello. No one is doing what I am doing. I am preeminent in my field."

The wine lubricated my spirit, the food witching, I didn't want to stop eating or drinking, so I let Jett do the talking, nodding from time to time to acknowledge my listening. His medium was antlers, horns, sometimes bone. Nature sculpture was what he termed it. From small arrangement to ten-foot tall free-forms. And he liked to incorporate gemstones, polished rock, copper, and sometimes silver.

"How do you get the antlers?" I asked between bites. "Do you hunt them?"

"I don't hunt for my art. Animals shed their antlers; others just die out there. Whatever has bone, it ends up as the last thing to remain in the scrublands. I've got a great collection. Big 12-point bucks, antlers like oak." Then he started talking about how he engraved them and ran molten copper in the etchings, how he gets real close to make sure he doesn't pour outside the groove, how patience and observation is important, intently focused on the changing fluid dynamics depending on the depth and width of the channel. His description of the process was detailed, I can't really remember much of it, but it brought him much joy.



His words started blurring after a while, I didn't really mind, I was enjoying my meal, and thought nothing of the aural disconnect. Then a dizziness started to spin, and my stomach twisted. I set aside my plate and wondered if I drank too much, but then, quickly, the dizziness straightened, nausea departed, and appetite returned. A cool comfort of calmness fell upon me. I recognized this feeling; I had experienced it many times before.

"Say, Jett." I interrupted. "Did you give me a dose of shrooms?"

"Whoa, Rich," replied Jett, and he set aside his plate, sat upright, got close and looked into my eyes. "I thought I made that clear." He thought a little, his lips twitched, and he wiped sweat away from his brow. He spoke solemnly and slow. "Now, yes, Rich, there are some magic mushrooms in the beans, and I should've made certain you understood. I thought you realized where you are. I apologize. But you are safe. Remain calm. The best thing to do is not to fret and worry, enjoy the surroundings, you got food and drink, relax."

He didn't have to tell me, I knew what to do, going into a trip with a wrong mindset dared dark outcomes. But it was nice of him to offer reassurance. "This is a very odd circumstance," I said. "Setting up in the middle of nowhere and giving people hallucinogens is a wild leisure activity you have, Jett."

"Ha, that's funny, I never thought of it like that." My jovial calm seemed to pass onto Jett, and he returned to his lounge position. "Sure am glad you have taken the serene approach. You know where you are, right?"

"I'm in the Alvord desert."

"Well, yes, in one sense. But you're also not."

"What?"

"There are places like elsewhere. Where the compass spins, time is not consistent, and the laws of science don't fit. Like the Bermuda Triangle and Easter Island. That's where you are now. In a vortex."

I didn't react.

"I'm here because you might say I'm a spirit guide."

"Oh." I thought about what he said. A vortex. It did feel different out here.

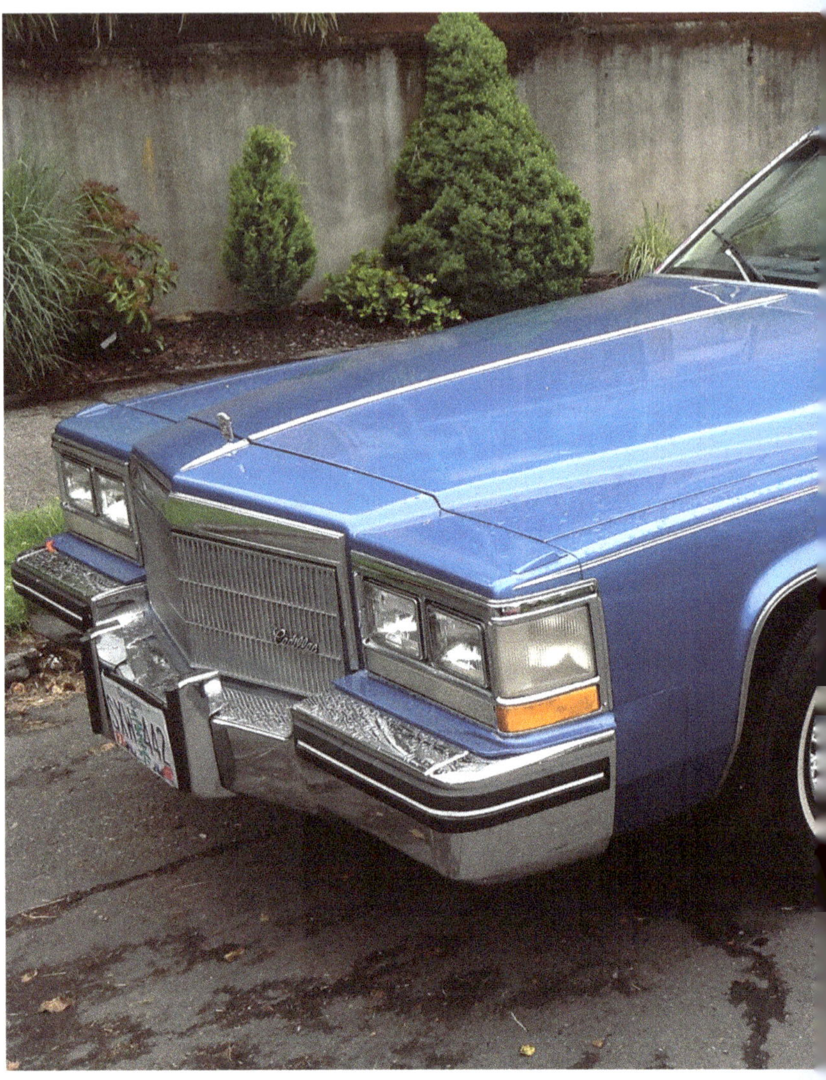

"Okay," and I thought about it some more. "That's even more odd, Jett. My spirit guide is a rancher from Wyoming."

Jett laughed, a laugh that was bigger than his body, the air around his face curved and rippled. It looked funny so I began to laugh, and the air waved and warbled around my laugh. "Oh, Rich, you're a hoot!" exclaimed Jett, slapping his knee. "You misunderstand. I am not your guide. I'm here for the car."

I stopped laughing to contemplate, but Jett laughed some more, a gold aura appeared around his body. "What do you mean?" I asked. "You're the spirit guide for the Caddy? That makes no sense. It's an inanimate object."

"Well, it's not. That car is rightly worried about you taking over the captain seat, and I am here to tell it that it will be fine, just fine, that you'll drive the car for a while, and that there will be more owners after you."

I was disappointed that I didn't have a guide, and Jett could tell. He got solemn and serious. "You," Jett said, pointing at my chest, "you don't need a spirit guide. You are singular, maybe the most singular

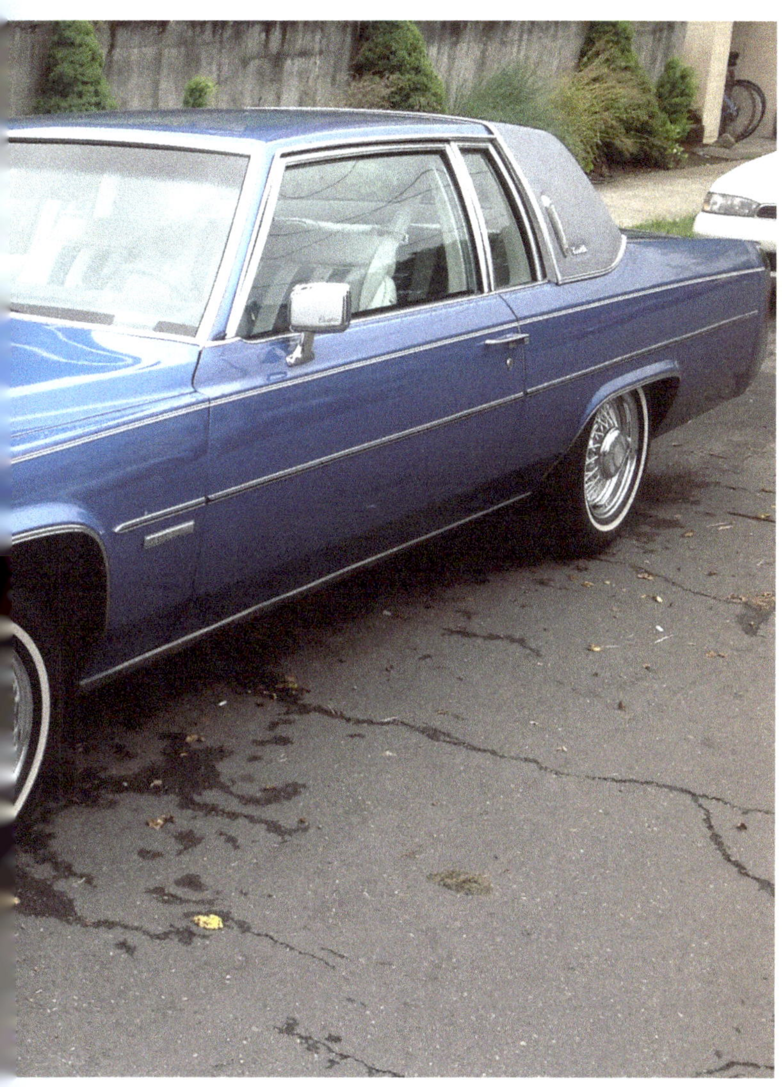

person that I have come across. I mean that in a good way, Rich. Like everything, it has its bad side but I'm saying you're singular in a good way. You don't need a guide." He then put on another Jimmie Rodgers record, made his way to the smoker, and prepared another platter of brisket and sausage. "Good brisket," he said. "That bundle of knotwood really leaves its mark."

I can't tell you what happened next. Something did. I have flashes of memory, brief remembrances that make little sense, but a thread of happiness and peace is what I remember most. For how long I was in this state I am not sure, but the next thing I recall I'm back in the driver's seat of the Caddy, rolling slow in the desert, and I'm yodeling. The steering is leaning to the right, and I don't see any sign of Jett or his barbecue trailer. I turned the wheel left for a wide circle to get my bearings. The sun was setting, the dark falling fast, the smell of smoke fading.

# Contributors

**Paisley Lee** (they/them) is a Portland-based artist whose practice and passions came from their love of old things. Since high school, Paisley has been inseparable from their film camera, and other analog interests do not trail far behind. With a specialty in portrait photography, Paisley brings a unique eye and sense of individualism to all of their work.
*IG: @paisley.jpeg*

**Sam Sangermano** (she/her) is a nail artist & photographer originally from Rhode Island and currently living in Portland, Oregon. Just a gal drifting through life preserving her experiences on film and making small treasures on people's nails. When she is not at the salon you can find her at the darkroom, studying Vietnamese, and on road trips looking for penny press machines.
*yournewfriendsam.com*
*IG: @dirtyneutron.nails*

**Zac Pranji** (he/they) is a visual artist and designer based in Portland who works mostly in collage and Riso print. They are inspired by architecture, phenomenology, and visual perception.
*IG: @zac_pranji*

**Hannah Love** (she/her) is a woman with a laptop from Portland, Oregon. When she is not working, she is practicing creative writing and befriending animals. Her work appears or is forthcoming in *Crow & Cross Keys*, *Across the Margin*, *Audience Askew Literary Journal*, and elsewhere.
*IG: @isthathannahlove*
*X: @hanniestew*

**S. Z. James** (he/him) is a writer living and ostensibly working in Portland, Oregon. He is currently at work on his debut novel. He has been published previously in *Deep Overstock* and *LURCH*. He is interested primarily in how people pretend to each other.

**John Kirkley** (he/him, b.1981) is a photographer based in Portland, Oregon. His photographic work observes an ever-changing landscape while navigating his place within it.
*johnconlonkirkley.com*
*IG: @yawnconlon*

**Andrew Simon** (he/him) teaches at an alternative high school in North Portland and is the co-owner and community director of Chess Club, an experiential retail shop in Old Town.

**Alex Diamond** (he/him) is a recent addition to Portland, hailing from Texas and New York. He has always maintained an art practice although does not have a formal arts education. His work is currently focused on a mixed casting/monoprinting process using mostly paper pulp. Diamond received a Bachelor of Architecture from the University of Texas at Austin and currently works in custom fabrication.
*alexjdiamond.com*
*IG: @alexjdiamond*

**Jamie Cattanach** (she/her) is a Florida-born writer based in Portland, Oregon. Her essays, poetry, and reportage have appeared or are forthcoming in *Nashville Review, Fourth Genre, SELF, Ms. Magazine, Willamette Week,* and many other outlets. She's a reader for the essays column at *The Rumpus* and the editor of the biweekly newsletter *Change of Heart.* Her work-in-progress memoir was chosen for the Tin House manuscript mentorship program in winter 2022.
*jamiecattanach.com*
*IG: @jamiecattanach*

**Christian Johnson** (he/him) is a Portland-based artist after almost two decades in New York City. His artistic inspirations are wide-ranging from figurative to abstract. The solitary figure in an abstract space is a universe.
*christianjohnson.com*
*IG: @christianjohnsonstudio*

**Ree Artemisa** (she/they/he) is a self-taught chicana artist. Their work focuses on themes of community, her heritage, BIPOC enjoying nature, and LGBTQIA representation. They currently live and work in Portland, Oregon.
*IG: @ree.artemisa*

**Anita Macauley** (she/her) holds an undergraduate degree in French from the University of Oregon and a Masters in Urban and Regional Planning from Portland State University. She rides a Trek and has lived in Portland since 1998.

**Goldandfaceted** (he/him) is a photographer who draws inspiration from everyday life in Portland. He seeks to capture the quiet dignity in familiar landscapes; To discover a divinity in the white noise as we trudge through daily ritual. Through his work, he invites viewers to appreciate the seemingly mundane.
*IG: @goldandfaceted*

**Tracey Nguyen** (she/they) is a Vietnamese-American poet and incoming law student.
*IG: @tr.ac.ey*

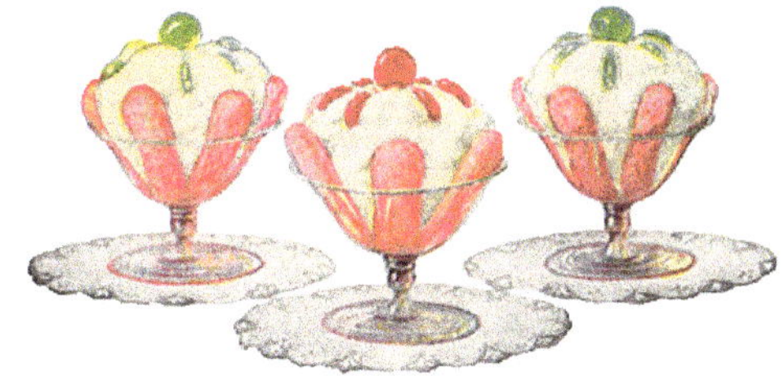

**Dustin Hendrick** (he/him) is a writer and filmmaker. He is the author of *The Endless M*, an autobiographical essay collection, and his short stories and essays have been featured in various literary journals. He was the recipient of a 2023 Oregon Literary Fellowship in fiction. By day he is a script supervisor and by night is at work on the dreaded novel. He lives in Portland, Oregon with his husband and fellow filmmaker Nathan Pacyna, with whom Dustin recently co-directed his first short film, the forthcoming *Out of View*, based on his short story of the same name.
*dustinhendrick.com*
*IG: @dustinunderscorehendrick*

**Sara Atwood** (she/her) is an Oregon-based writer and a writing/literature instructor at Portland State University and Pacific Northwest College of Art. She also leads Delve Readers' Seminars for Portland Literary Arts. Her academic work has been published in numerous journals including *Nineteenth-Century Prose* and *The Journal of Pre-Raphaelite Studies*. She has published a book, *Ruskin's Educational Ideals* (Ashgate 2011), and numerous book chapters. She is currently working on a memoir.
*linkedin.com/in/sara-lussier-atwood-82b8b82*

**Kimberlee Frederick** (she/her) is a collage artist preoccupied with the dreamy, surreal, and occasionally terrifying experience of having a body. She lives in and rarely leaves SE Portland.
*kimberleefrederick.com*
*IG: @unrealcitypdx*

**Noelle Smith** (she/her) writes about her obsessions and the thoughts that keep her up at night. She has periodically traveled the country as a street poet over the last ten years. Her essays currently reside on substack.
*noellesmith.art*
*noellesmith.substack.com*

**Claire Gunville** (she/her, b. Seattle, Washington) is a visual artist, printmaker, and educator based in Portland, Oregon. By employing used and outdated electronic items, her work ruminates on the ways in which humans have impacted our global ecology through technological advancements. Her work has been shown at Blackfish Gallery, MRKT Gallery, and Carnation Contemporary. Claire works as the gallery assistant to Nucleus Portland and teaches community art classes at Daffodill Studios. She received her BFA in Printmaking from Pacific Northwest College of Art.
*IG: @clairegunville*

**Emily Moon** (she/her) is a queer transgender poet from Portland, Oregon. She is author of *It's Just You & Me, Miss Moon*, editor at First Matter Press, host for the Eastside Poetry Workshop, and host for the Queerlandia Open Mic. Her work includes recent appearances in *Drip Lit* and *Rogue Agent*.
*linktr.ee/EmilyMoonPoet*
*IG: @emilymoonpoet*
*FB: Emily.Moon.57*

**Megan Chin** (she/they) is a mixed-race Chinese American visual artist who earned a BFA in Painting from the Maryland Institute College of Art while concentrating on gender studies. She has been an artist-in-residence at the Macedonia Institute in Chatham, New York as well as at the Vermont Studio Center in Johnson, Vermont. In 2020, they exhibited work in the de Young Open exhibition at the Fine Arts Museum of San Francisco. Chin is a community member of the organization Anti-capitalism for Artists and has organized the Anti-capitalism Artists Book Club in Portland.
*meganchinart.com*
*IG: @meganchinart*

**Jack Wang** (he/him) is a writer hailing from The North Star State. A graduate of Lewis & Clark College, he currently lives with his wife and white shepherd in NE Portland. An Americanist in sensibility, Jack takes inspiration from modern and contemporary writers, forging his own experiences within a national aesthetic expression. When he isn't scribbling, he enjoys rugby, music, and coffee.
*cloudedprose.substack.com*

**Judy Jiang** (she/her) was born and raised in Oregon in a home with her parents, grandfather, and three siblings. Her writing and photography can be found in *Oregon Humanities* and elsewhere. Judy seeks to deeply understand and embody life at both its most emotional depths and its most transcendent peaks. She is currently at work on a memoir on daughterhood and loss.
*judyonpaper.com*
*IG: @judytakesphotos*

**Maxwell Kline** (they/he) was born in Gresham, but grew up in the foothills of Boise. They have tamed several packs of coyotes and spent much time photosynthesizing with Big Sagebrush. Currently, they are raising a clutch of sage grouse chicks in Portland, Oregon, as well as attending Portland State University. They are pursuing degrees in Creative Writing and Environmental studies. Kline has been published previously in *LURCH* and *Pathos Litmag*.
*maxie.rodeo*

**Alicia Johnson** (she/her) is an ALM candidate for Harvard Extension School's Creative Writing and Literature program. A native of Portland, she currently lives in Sandy with her husband and five boys. When she isn't at her computer writing, she enjoys adventuring with her family and supporting their many musical endeavors.
*IG: @aliciajohnsonauthor*

**Stephanie Hatch** (she/her) is a contemporary artist, currently residing in SW Washington. Stephanie grew up in the beautiful wooded hills of Southern Oregon, and a love for nature and cosmic powers live in her work because of it. Memories of children's movies from the 80s (e.g. *Return to Oz, The Hugga Bunch*) and Lisa Frank color palettes are alive and well in Hatch's art. Through collage and paint she creates surreal landscapes in which she seeks to rediscover her childhood sense of wonder, joy, and belief in fantastic possibilities.
*stephaniehatch.com*
*IG: @stephaniemariehatch*

# HONOR ROLL

Nancy Neighbor Russell

Larry Supnet

Bill Walton

Saint Gertrude of Nivelles

the crows

Oregon Historical Society

Harlee Case

Brianna, George, & Ene

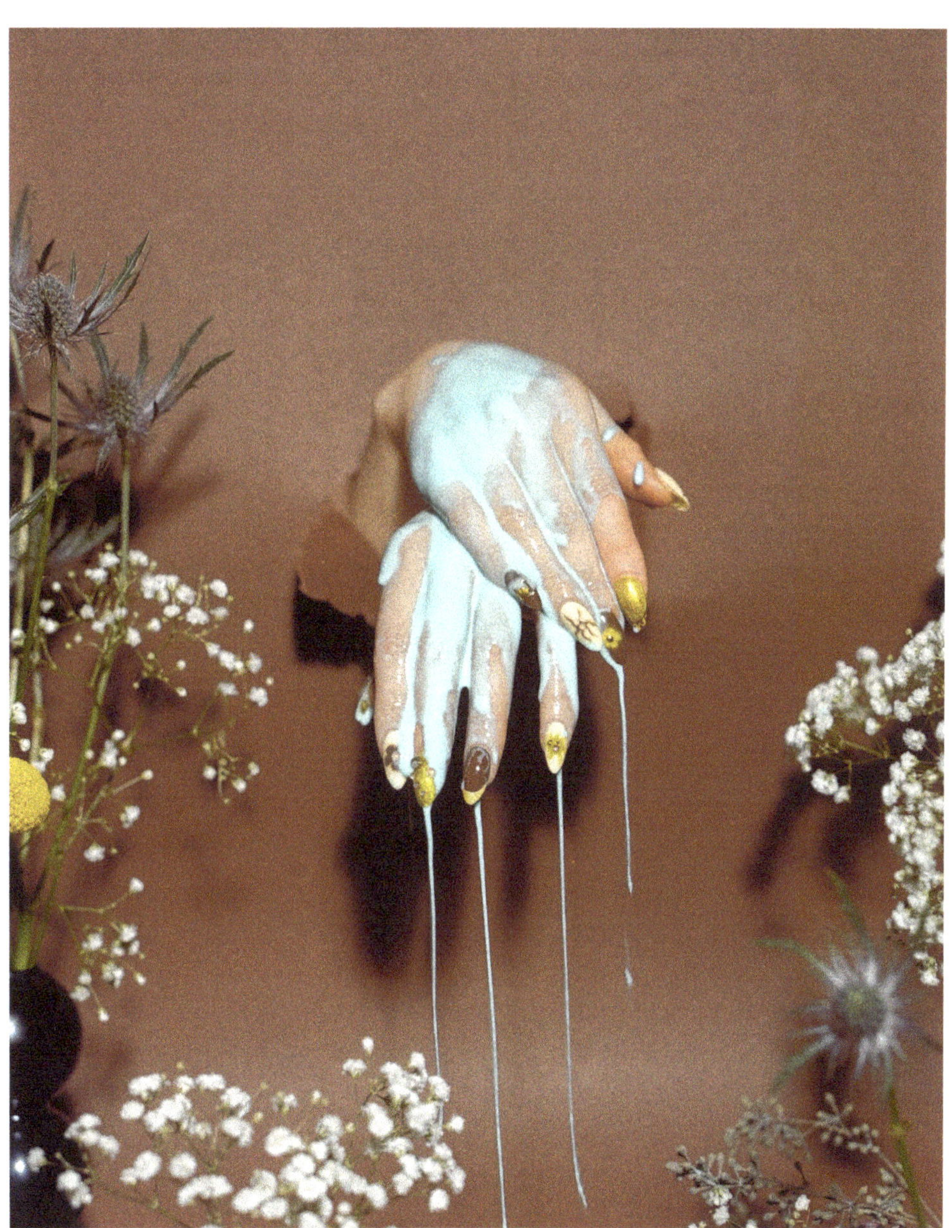

# M O R E
## from Buckman

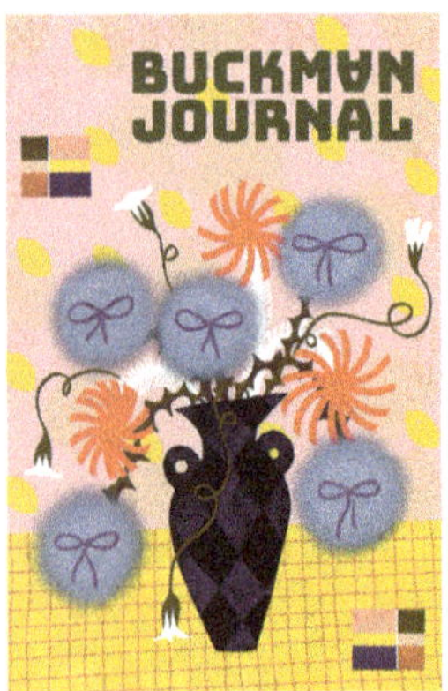
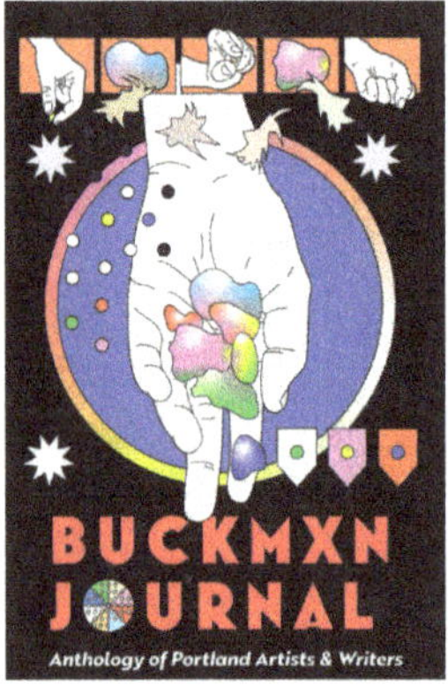
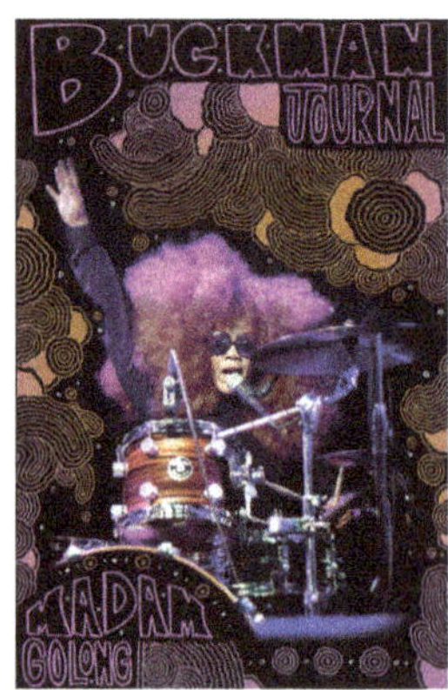

*Buckman Journal*

*Buckmxn Journal* is a vehicle. An anthology inspired by and made to showcase Portland's literary and artistic talent. Each biannual issue collects the creativity at work in our city and packs full-color pages with the work of over 25 local writers and artists across all genres. With a recognition from the Independent Publishers Book Awards, *Buckmxn Journal* is here to keep print media alive and kicking.

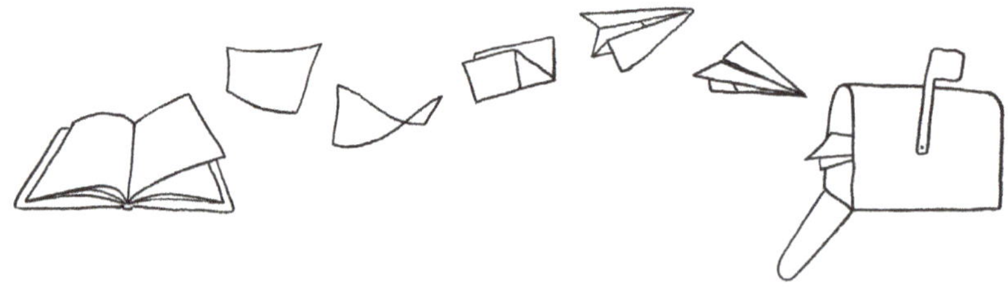

*Buckmxn Story Service*

With the power of the U.S. Postal Service, Buckmxn delivers to your door one story a week for ten weeks. It's like a story of the week club featuring the finest writers on the scene, curated by the crew at Buckmxn.

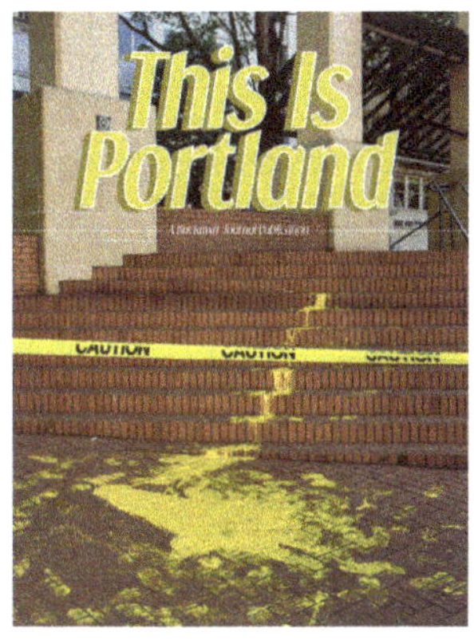

*This is Portland*
A travel guide tells you where to go and what to eat. *This is Portland* goes further. By presenting the city's acclaimed artists and writers, as well as its unique cultural innovators, this book conveys the soul and spirit of Portland like no other.

*The Great Gatsby: Buckman Critical Edition*
Words by F. Scott Fitzgerald, Merridawn Duckler, Emmi Greer, & Rich Perin
Art by Ellen Robinette

Buckman's Gatsby features the original novel accompanied by illustrations and essays that engage a 21st century appreciation of the American classic.

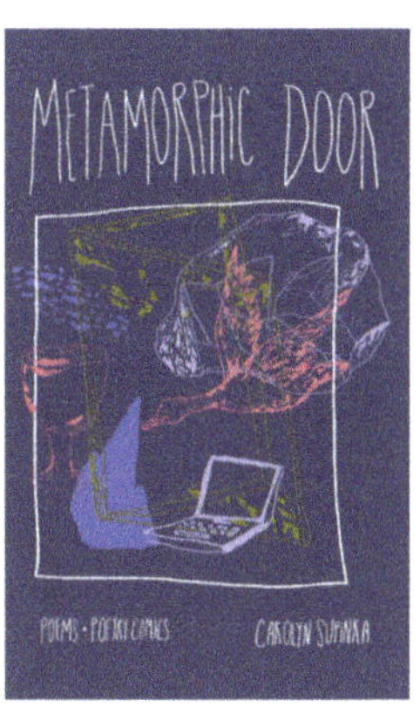

*Metamorphic Door*
Words & Art by Carolyn Supinka

In this debut poetry collection, stone flows, air becomes geese, time and light intersect and split. Pacific Northwest poet and artist Carolyn Supinka delivers the quakes and tectonic shifts via poems, illustrations, and the blending of the two, poetry comics.

*Tiny Haiku*
Words by Daniel O'Brien-Bravi
Art by Ellen Robinette

Barista Haiku that graced the blackboard of Tiny's Coffee in Portland, OR, weekly from 2014-2017. Darkly funny, playful, and modern verse accompanied with full-color illustrations, as well as images of the original haikus on the Tiny's blackboard. This is poetry for fellow service industry workers, and all who survived the last chaotic decade.

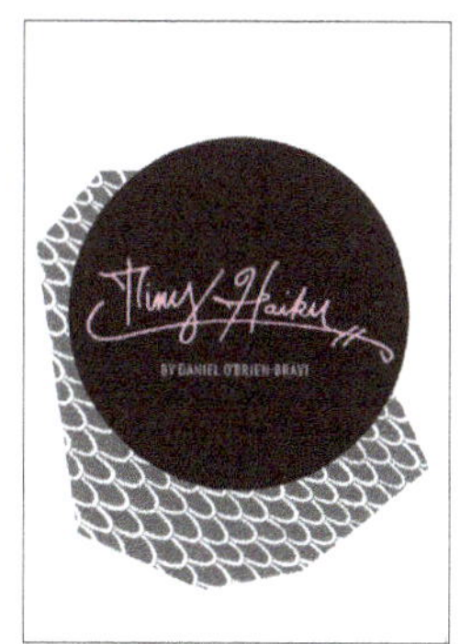

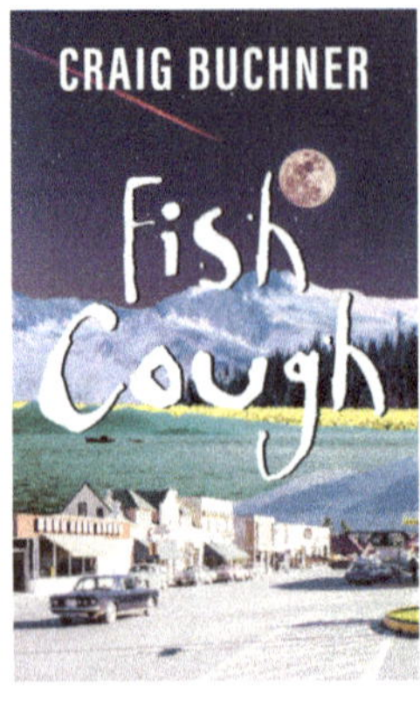

*Fish Cough*
Words By Craig Buchner
Art by Emmi Greer

During a once-every-33-years meteor shower, an evil unlike anything on earth crashes into a tree in a Portland backyard, setting off a string of puzzling and unsettling events— beginning with the appearance of an anthropomorphic squirrel named Gordito and an invisible presence capable of mind-control.

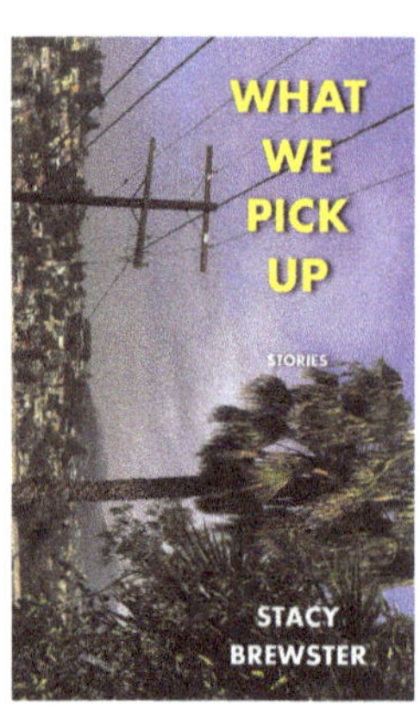

*What We Pick Up*
Words & art by Stacy Brewster

*What We Pick Up* is the debut story collection from Portland author and screenwriter Stacy Brewster, recipient of the 2019 Literary Arts Fellowship in Drama. These eleven stories span vastly different decades and landscapes but all manage to mix dark humor, cinematic detail, and sharp prose that turns clichés of boyhood and manhood on their heads.

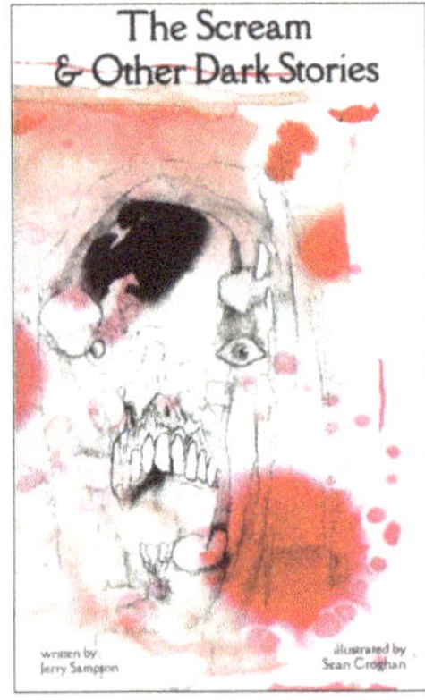

*The Scream & Other Dark Stories*
Words by Jerry Sampson
Art by Sean Croghan

Deep in the shadows of the human soul are monsters that should never see the light of day. But some fight to the surface, consume the entire being, then prey on anyone else that is around. This is the world of new horror. Artist Sean Croghan provides eerie illustrations.

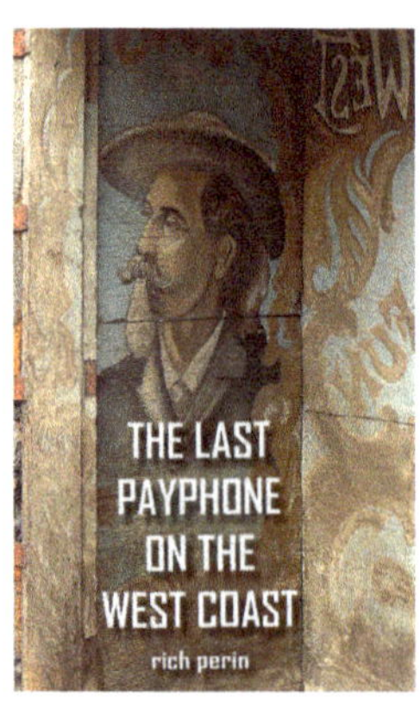

*The Last Payphone on the West Coast*
Words & art by Rich Perin

*The Last Payphone on the West Coast* is a short story collection of rare realness—centered around folks finding analog moments amongst the age of instantaneous expectation. Told with a tint of the surreal, the twelve stories wander around the North American continent, and are deeply alive with the people that reside in them.

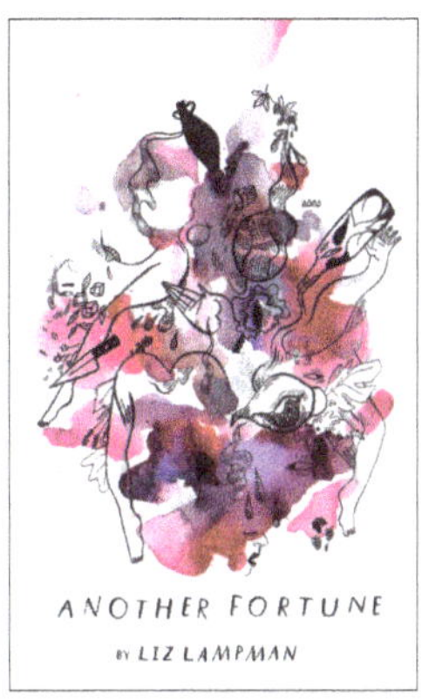

*Another Fortune & Other Poems*
Words by Elizabeth Rivers
Art by Lettie Jane Rennekamp

These boozy poems drip with a queer wisdom, and are anchored by a heroic crown of sonnets. With juicy, emotive watercolors by illustrator Lettie Jane Rennekamp, *Another Fortune* is sure to sweep sweep you up into its luxurious language and sensory reverie.

*20!8: the Order of Athena vs. the Orange Bastard*
By Anita Lobo
Art by Hugh Newell

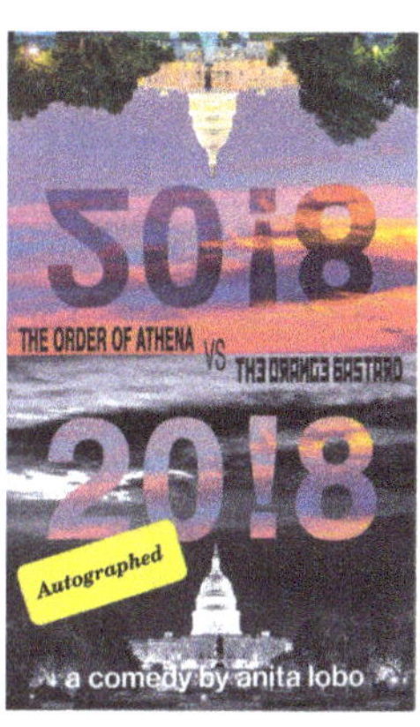

Imagine a world in which the title of president gets nowhere near Donald J. Tr***. This version of the world is possible only with the help of a secret order of politically and pantsuit-inclined female assassins. *20!8* is an absurdist comedy for anyone who has wondered if we are living in a glitch in the space-time continuum.

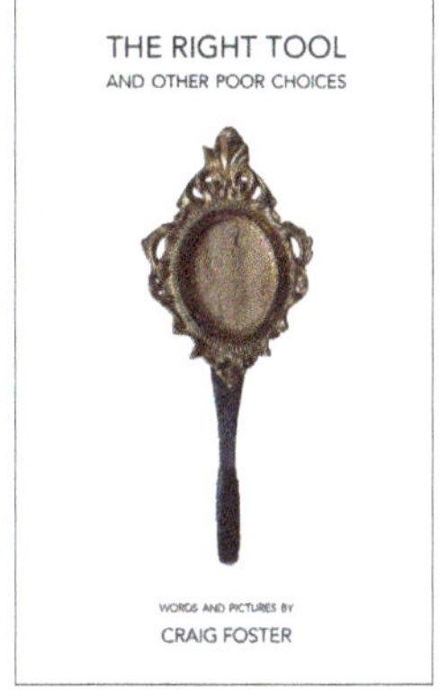

*The Right Tool & Other Poor Choices*
Words & Art by Craig Foster

In twenty-three flash fiction stories, Foster presents a succession of bewildered psyches. The quick delivery makes *The Right Tool* the perfect book to crack open when you need an instant dose of someone else's strange. The author also provides illustrations.

Find all these titles, and more at **buckmanjournal.com**!

Keep an eye out for these forthcoming books in 2024:

*In the Frail* by Erinn Kathryn
*Somewhere in Another Place* by Mike Vos
*Many Seasons* by Frances Badalamenti & Aaron Wessling
*Rain or Coincidences* by Xinyu Liu
*Buckman Journal 013: Preserve & Decay*